EVERY PARENT'S CALLING

to educate and disciple their child

Ellen Schuknecht

RIVERSTONE GROUP
PUBLISHING

As Christian parents, we want our children rooted in a foundation of God's love and truth. We desire to connect and remain influential in their lives, but we can become increasingly concerned in a culture that attempts to erode the long-standing pillars of our country — faith and family. Mrs. Schuknecht provides intensely practical and insightful encouragement for both moms and dads, and she offers valuable guidance to rearing challenging children in challenging times.

Here's What Leaders Are Saying about This Resource...

Ellen beautifully articulates the power in answering God's call to teach our children. Whether shaping their hearts through modeling virtuous behavior or guiding them through the peaks and valleys of learning new skills, Ellen outlines thoughtful and loving ways to disciple our children while encouraging them to grow into the people who God designed them to be.

— **Randan Steinhauser**
education reform advocate & parent

In *Every Parent's Calling,* author Ellen Schuknecht shares a lifetime of wisdom, experience and practical advice that will equip parents to raise Godly children in these difficult and challenging times. Mother, teacher, mentor, school administrator, grandmother and author, Ellen speaks with authority and writes with conviction and deep faith. Her book should be a primary resource for every parent and teacher dedicated to Christian education.

— **Michael Chrasta, Ph.D.,**
Advisor to UMSI
author of *Make It a Place of Springs*

The knowledge and wisdom Ellen Schuknecht sets forth in *Every Parent's Calling* is not a compilation of abstract theories. Rather, the principles and practices contained in this book were forged in the crucible of life as Ellen passionately pursued the mission of training "life-equipped disciples of the Lord Jesus Christ for the next generation." Some would say Ellen earned "street cred" in her roles as mother and grandmother as well as parent trainer and coordinator of the Veritas Family Ministry Program. I agree.

In my more than 50 years as a public and private education professional – including 20 years as NAUMS, Inc. Chief Executive Officer, I can say unequivocally that the University-Model® is the most effective model of education. In addition, I can affirm without hesitation that Ellen Schuknecht knows the University-Model® well and has proven to be one of the most dedicated, knowledgeable and passionate authors and parent educators I have known.

— **Barbara Nicholson Freeman, M.ED.**
CEO of NAUMS, Inc.

I'm so glad a whole chapter is devoted to dads. Glen's personal stories, own admissions and suggestions are powerful.... Chapter four about words was a favorite.... The section on the power of words to unify or divide is a good reminder to all of our parents, and the questions listed should serve as a helpful reminder to all of us.... The chapter on parenting and teaching the difficult child is something I wish I would have had when my three were little. Nice job on describing what each of these types looks like and how to respond.... The personal examples are really helpful. I also liked the inclusion of your personal testimony and those of other families.

— **Starrla Fowler**
Founding member of Veritas Academy

DEDICATION

I dedicate *Every Parent's Calling* to my kind husband, Glen, who patiently encouraged me through the many months it took to complete this book. I also dedicate *Every Parent's Calling* to Joey, Kate, Jude, Hadassah, Greta, Will, Isaac, Elsie, Asa, Alma and Bethlehem — my grandchildren, who continue to inspire and teach me so much. Finally, I dedicate this book to my adult children and their spouses, who are a joy to walk out life with. God has blessed me with a family, who I dreamed of as a young girl; and I am deeply grateful for you all.

EVERY PARENT'S CALLING TO EDUCATE AND DISCIPLE THEIR CHILD

Copyright © 2022 Ellen Schuknect. All rights reserved.

Riverstone Group, LLC – Jasper, Georgia, USA

Riverstone Group Publishing

Softcover: ISBN: 978-1-7346235-8-1

All Scripture quotations are from The Holy Bible, English Standard Version. ESV® Text Edition: 2016. Copyright © 2001 by Crossway Bibles, a publishing ministry of Good News Publishers.

CONTENTS

INTRODUCTION

Certain experiences and thoughts I held as a child still stand as vivid images in my mind. I remember how my brother and I would crawl around on all fours — deep in our forested property, searching for an elusive four-leaf clover. Having read a story about how a four-leaf clover would bring hope, faith, love and luck, I dreamed of a life that would come true if I were lucky enough to find one. I don't recall succeeding, but I remember the hopes and dreams that were attached to this endeavor — that of becoming a mom someday, of having a loving family of my own. Even as a child, I longed to be a mother — so I turned to mothering my siblings! You can imagine how that worked! I often have pondered if this deep longing rose out of a need to be loved and cherished by my parents ,who were too busy to notice the needs of their children or nurture a relationship with us.

With 300 acres of farm and forest land in Northwest Oregon — as well as an attorney's practice to maintain, my dad was consumed with work and providing for his family. My mom was a buzz of activity from morning until bedtime, tending to orchards, berry fields, gardens, farm animals — and five children. We learned to work hard, but we also chose to stay clear of her path — whenever possible — to avoid being given more work to do.

It was an idyllic life in many ways. We built forts and forged trails through the forests, which contained brooks and ponds filled with crawdads and trout. We rode our horse through the hay fields, picked fruit from the orchard trees and ate handfuls of berries right off the bushes. We constructed rope swings in the barn lofts. Technology consisted of a small black-and-white TV, a manual typewriter and one telephone on a shared community line with neighbors — one of which was my grandmother, who loved to listen in on our phone conversations.

I wonder today how these early experiences shaped me as a wife, mom and now grandmother. As I think back to my childhood, the temporary nature of life becomes a reality. Author Gloria Naylor stated, "Time is a funny thing. I was always puzzled how a single day could stretch itself out to eternity in your mind — all the while years melted down into the fraction of a second."[1]

Hunting for that rare four-leaf clover still stands as a clear memory because it symbolizes a lifelong journey, searching after true meaning and value in life. I remember contemplating eternity as a child and wondering what God was like. My imaginations took me to places beyond my small world. Even as a child, I wanted my life to matter, to be about something meaningful.

God Has Not Changed

Much has changed in my life since those young days. Much has changed in the world as well, but God has not changed. Nor have His aims for mankind. He is the same yesterday, today and forever. (Hebrews 13:8) Mankind is still *Imago Dei* — created in God's Image. This longing for something grand is built into our hearts by our Creator so that we will seek Him. The Gospel is precious Good News, and the Cross of Christ is unfathomably beautiful. What the world offers will never meet what the hearts of we or our children long for. That is why we must lead them in practices that form their imaginations, hearts and minds around loftier ideals built on eternal truth — truth they were created to embrace.

> *"Just as a plane is made to fly, a book is made to be read and a fish is made to swim, our purpose is to image and glorify God. If we hope to thrive as individuals and as a society, we must live in alignment with that design. Otherwise, we are fighting, not just against God, but against our very natures."*[2]
>
> — John Stonestreet

It's no different for this generation than it was in earlier centuries or for me as a child. In his address to the men in Athens, Paul had much to say to a group of religious men, who were always looking for some new thought or activity in their search for a relationship with God. Searching for something new — like a four-leaf clover — can feel exciting to our students today as well. Yet what their souls need — and even long for — is a deep dive into the timeless truths of Scripture. As Paul spoke in the Areopagus, he said:

> *"And he made from one man every nation of mankind to live on all the face of the earth, having determined allotted periods and the boundaries of their dwelling place, that they should seek God, and perhaps feel their way toward him and find him. Yet he is actually not far from each one of us, for 'in him we live and move and have our being.'"*
>
> Acts 17:25-27a

In our world today, alternate world realities clash with increasing vengeance, forming confusion and mass division. Carl R. Trueman wrote, "*The task of the Christian is not to whine about the moment in which he or she lives but to understand its problems and respond appropriately to them.*"[3] As Christian parents, therefore, we must seek to understand the culture in which our children are growing up and teach them to respond wisely. The Christian reality maintains that God created the world with meaning and order. And He created each individual on purpose for a purpose to be discovered. The opposing view is that no such providential meaning or order exists — that everyone must determine their meaning, identity and purpose. In this reality, life shrinks down to ME and MY rights, but it's a dead end and one that leads to despair because we were not created to live merely for ourselves. When we remove our nation's proclamation of individual liberty from under the covering and direction of a higher being, our culture shrinks to chaos and disorder. When my governance replaces His order and governance, my life shrinks to the pursuit of personal desires and also morality becomes a matter of taste and not truth. In this scenario, I am required to take on the weighty responsibility of designing my ethics and knowledge, leaving me gasping for the true, good and beautiful but having no idea where to find them. In this realm, our children's very breath of life is obstructed. No wonder that anxiety is pandemic today — even in young children.

My hunt for the four-leaf clover was a yearning for something true, good and beautiful — and for God who created it all. I tried to fulfill this longing in many other ways — through academia, trying to please others, striving to be the perfect mom and wife, gaining material possessions and wealth; but each became a dead-end. In fact, they merely increased the longing for something lasting and real. Only the one, true God, who created it all, can meet this deepest need in our hearts.

Our Culture Is Under Rapid Change

Back just seven years ago, when my daughter Erin and I wrote *Free to Parent* thoughts of a worldwide pandemic were nonexistent. That we would be required to wear masks in public? Surreal! Contact tracing? Social distancing? Zoom meetings and virtual learning? We would not have imagined it. Last year, millions of Texans were shocked with the loss of power and water due to snow and ice storms — an occurrence that would have seemed out of a science-fiction movie. Add to that the absurd political and social unrest. Everything seems to be shaking. Anxiety feels normative, casting a wider, tighter net and extending its tenacious grip on younger and younger children. Isolation, fear of illness and death, loss of jobs, social unrest plus disruption to normal routines all have led to a high degree of mental distress for both adults and children. In the face of these uncertain and ever-changing times, how do we rear, guide and educate our children?

Another culture shift is that the undergirding of our culture — the pillars of family and church, which for so long have been the glue — are weakening. I am profoundly grateful for University-Model® schools, which continue to swim upstream by steadfastly holding to Biblical truth; while they partner with parents, viewing them as primary and supporting them in their God-ordained roles. Mom and Dad, you are the most important and most influential people in your children's lives! What happens in your family is far more significant than what happens outside it. Impactful discipleship occurs within your homes as you learn to work together, worship God together and come to understand how He has uniquely positioned each of you to be His light in a confused and hurting culture.

How Did We Get Here?

How did our nation get to this place of disturbing disunity? It seems to me that deceptive ideas, which have been brewing for quite some time, are being consumed now by large numbers in large quantities. We may be living in the time to which Paul referred in 2 Timothy 4:3-4 — *"For the time is coming when people will not endure sound teaching, but having itching ears they will accumulate for themselves teachers to suit their own passions, and will turn away from listening to the truth...."*

Jesus warned that *"many false prophets will arise and lead many astray"* (Matthew 24:11). Likewise, Jude cautioned believers to be wary of false teachers, referring to them as *hidden reefs*, which served to destroy ships in his time; as *shepherds feeding themselves;* as *waterless clouds swept along by the winds*, promising refreshment but not delivering; as *fruitless trees in late autumn;* as *wild waves of the sea casting up the foam of their shame;* and as *wandering stars* giving deceptive guidance. From prison, Peter concluded his final epistle to the church with a strong exhortation to not be carried away with the error of lawless people, who twist Scripture to their destruction — as doing so would result in the loss of stability.

As a teen, I remember being drawn to the lure of so-called freedom in *"doing whatever felt good to me and being whoever I wanted me to be."* These are ideals espoused by Friedrich Nietzsche, whose influence remains prevalent today. He strongly advocated for individuals to "create" themselves and

11

throw away any concept of morality that a Creator would impose on them. Sound familiar? These ideas led me to a yearlong state of despair in college. Gratefully, I was confronted with the Gospel and had to make a choice about which truths to base my life on. I chose Jesus. Where did Nietzsche's ideas land him? He suffered a psychotic breakdown at the age of 44 and never recovered.

However, I continued to think that achieving my full potential rested primarily upon my performance and efforts. In hindsight, I see how these ideas had roots in false teaching from philosophers like Karl Marx, who believed that religion was what kept people from reaching their full potential; that for human beings to be fully human, they need to stop giving glory to God and instead ascribe this glory to themselves. (The first chapter of Romans warns of this very thing.) To Karl Marx, the removal of religion was essential for citizens to find true happiness. Karl Marx also died a destitute and broken man.

Finally, there are Darwin's ideals, who strived to remove teleology (the doctrine of design and purpose in the world) from nature and, thus, from human beings as well. Yet, with no God-given beginning or destiny, we have no transcendent moral standards or virtues to which we need to conform. Carl R. Trueman, author of *The Rise and Triumph of the Modern Self,* has given me much to ponder regarding how false teachers — through the ages — have led us to where we are today. He states that "*the social imaginary is thoroughly permeated by the ideas of these three men, or at least the implications thereof.*" He goes on to write: "*When teleology is dead and self-creation is the name of the game, then the present moment and the pleasure it can contain become the keys to eternal life.*" [3]

Called to Purposefully Parent

Your children's life stories are being shaped and built right now in your home amidst this culture. What you do and who you are matter greatly.

You are God's anointed in their lives and their most valuable influence. Every day, by your words and actions, you build identity and purpose into your children. I believe that God has blessed many of you with uniquely strong-willed children — boys and girls who want to lead and are not easily persuaded to follow. Their God-given strengths may be just what will prevent them from following false teaching. I am especially drawn to these stubborn, determined children because I see so much potential for them to become future leaders for God's Kingdom. However, I do realize how exasperated parents can feel when they wind up in daily battles with their stubborn, passionate, driven boys and girls who refuse to comply. If you have such children, be grateful.

Our culture needs men and women who are not easily swayed or molded. These future leaders must be nurtured thoughtfully, guided wisely and taught how to compassionately engage their culture — yet without compromising God's truth. Jesus built His ministry around youths who went on to build His Church. I believe the young people of today will redeem their peer culture. And not just the strong-willed! All children can become the messengers of hope to their generation when empty pursuits fail. That is what this book is about — a call to parent this generation of children with purpose and wisdom; to focus on what matters most; to teach our children to root their thinking and their lives in the eternal, unchanging truths of God's Word; to establish that the Bible is not just another source of knowledge but the true source of wisdom; and to make our voices heard above the constant stream of voices they hear through Google, social media platforms and digital entertainment.

We are called to live with purpose as parents in our marriages, our homes and our careers. From prison, the Apostle Paul urged believers to *"to walk in a manner worthy of the calling to which you have been called, with all humility and gentleness, with patience, bearing with one another in love"* (Ephesians 4:1-2). Only as we walk in God's calling on our lives will we find lasting significance. University-Model® Schools call for a return to the Deuteronomy 6 Mandate:

> *"'You shall love the LORD your God with all your heart and with all your soul and with all your might. And these words that I command you today shall be on your heart. You shall teach them diligently to your children, and shall talk of them when you sit in your house, and when you walk by the way, and when you lie down, and when you rise'"*
> (Deuteronomy 6:5-7).

This lifestyle mandate is a call to walk with our children, educating and discipling them in such a manner that they will be drawn irresistibly to Jesus so that they will find the fulfillment for which they long in the knowledge and love of God who created each of them. They won't find it in seeking temporary happiness and pleasures — or by being self-absorbed. They won't find it in luck or fame or fortune. Nor will they find it in their performance — no matter how good it is. They will find it in the very life of Jesus. Only with Jesus will they find lasting joy and contentment — and authentic relevance.

Our Calling as Parents

CHAPTER ONE

Called to What Matters Most

"The greatest legacy one can pass on to one's children and grandchildren is not money or other material things accumulated in one's life, but rather a legacy of character and faith."[5]

— Billy Graham

Even as a young girl, I dreamed of the day when I would become a mom. My deep longing for something significant always came down to the idea of someday being a mom within a warmly connected family. God already was planning in my heart a sense that the relationship between parents and their children were of vital importance. Having completed a major in psychology and an education degree with an emphasis in child development, I considered myself equipped to write a book on parenting — even before I had any children. My three children quickly humbled my ambitions, however; and instead, I immersed myself into the challenge of rearing them.

Once a lifelong Oregonian, I never would have imagined leaving the clover-covered hills and forests of my childhood for what I perceived to be dry, hot, brown, flat Texas. Yet my entire family — the one I longed for and envisioned as a child — now resides in Austin, Texas, where we walk out life together, rearing our family's next generation within a University-Model® community. I didn't need to find a four-leaf clover. I needed to seek and find Jesus, and I discovered His calling for me.

Called to Lasting Relationships with Your Children

I wrote *Free to Parent* in 2014 when three of my grandkids were attending Veritas Academy. My aim was to help parents replace practices that stood in the way of connected, healthy relationships with ones that fostered strong, lasting bonds. Deep inside, I knew that the key to a parent's influence with their children rested in healthy relationships. My aim in writing the book was to help parents move past the stumbling blocks that frustrated their attempts to guide and teach their children. Plus, I was personally experiencing how these frustrations stood in the way of progress during the school days at home with my grandchildren.

Teaching my grandkids has taught me a great deal. In *Chapter Five* of this book, I have included chapters on specific relationship issues that commonly crop up during the school days at home. These chapters include helpful suggestions for how to effectively work and connect with children, who behave in ways that make teaching and rearing them a challenge. These suggestions are derived not only from my experience with 11 unique grandkids but also from mentoring and walking with hundreds of parents over the years.

In *Free to Parent,* my daughter Erin wrote, "*A disconnected heart impulsively withdraws.*" She went on to say, "*We must establish a connection that runs from our heart to our child's heart to communicate effectively. Otherwise, our communication, whatever it is, largely remains undeliverable.*" I am even more convinced today that our influence takes place via warm relational attachment. I know that, after calling out 10-year-old Will for some misbehavior, I must intentionally weave our hearts back together again for him to receive — or even hear — anything I have to say. He will not believe me unless he feels connected to me. He will not listen to me if I have not taken the time to listen to him. Belonging and attachment set up influence.

This past spring, I decided to celebrate the end of the 2020-21 school year with my Thursday grandkid group by walking with them to a small local store for a treat. I gave them clear instructions on what they could pick from and how to behave, and they quietly and quickly picked out their treats. Except for one granddaughter who could not decide!

After paying for everyone else's treats, I grew impatient as she tried to explain what she wanted. We eventually left the store — upset with each other. Without stopping to listen, I began to lecture her. *"Did you really have to keep us all waiting over a treat?"* However, I also sensed that I was overreacting. Wondering if I had misunderstood my granddaughter, I put my arm around her in an effort to reengage with her. At this point, she wanted nothing to do with me and pulled away. She needed for me to admit my impatient reaction before she could see her issue and learn from this experience. Later, we had a great conversation; but it took intentional effort on my part to hear her, validate how I made her feel and then forge a renewed attachment between her heart and mine.

Our children need us to listen to them before offering correction or even encouragement. That day, I was on a mission to get back home; and I lacked the patience to perceive what was really going on. When my granddaughter proclaimed, *"You didn't hear me,"* she was correct. I made a false assumption and ran with it. I was so focused on what I wanted that I failed to hear what was being said to me.

I am reminded of Jesus when He healed the woman who had been suffering with a discharge of blood for 12 years. Although He was surrounded by a crowd and headed to Jairus's house to heal his daughter, He sensed that someone had touched His garments. Instead of forging forward, He stopped and listened to the woman tell Him her *whole story*. He listened to her — despite His busy agenda — before offering her life-giving words.

Listening gives us insights into what a child is feeling, so we can validate their pain before offering guidance. Listening tills and softens the hearts of our children to receive words of both encouragement and correction. Listening to our children is a key to gaining lasting, influential relationships with them.

Our entire Christian experience is rooted in relational connection with God and with others. Each of us is born with a God-given need to be known, loved and valued for who we are – without fear of rejection. Brain research shows the centers that regulate emotions, character and even identity are all relational. Therefore, these centers respond best to interactions with others — receiving comfort from someone when hurt, being greeted with joy, commended for a job well done. Who better to gain these from than one's mom and dad! The degree to which your children will be vulnerable with you — concerning their messy places — is directly related to how connected they feel with you at a heart level. Children need the security that comes with knowing their mom and dad will go through anything with them, that they are not alone as they face hardships — even those they have brought on themselves.

Thankfully, Jesus is our ultimate security because He is the bridge by which we connect with God. He loves us right where we are — even in our brokenness.

Called to Secure Foundations

As I consider all of the families God has allowed me to walk with over the years, a few fundamental principles rise to the top that our children (and we) must grasp to flourish and thrive in our culture. We want our children to stand strong when the rains fall and the floods come and the winds blow and beat upon them. We want their lives founded on the Rock. (Matthew 7:24-25)

A life founded on the Rock begins with knowing God! It almost sounds cliche. Yet it's indispensably fundamental for a transformed life. A.W. Tozer stated in *The Knowledge of the Holy*, "*A low view of God is the cause of a hundred lesser evils. A high view of God is the solution to ten thousand temporal problems.*"[6] Our eternal purpose evolves around knowing and loving God — and the way to find Him is through Jesus, who is "*the way, and the truth, and the life.*"

When this telos is disregarded and replaced instead with a random view of God and the meaning of life, we are left to create our meaning and way. However, we were not created for these burdens; and trying to carry them ends in brokenness and despair. It always does!

I had begun to enter this very slippery slope in my sophomore year of college. As a psychology major in the 1970s, who was taught by professors who promoted ideas like the ones mentioned earlier, I was reading a tall stack of books built on false precepts. These ideas led me into a very troubling, dark time during which anxious thoughts and ideas whirled — without restraint — in my mind. Instead of a future hope, my thoughts spun about past mistakes. If I was responsible for making my meaning and purpose, I grew worried that my future already was ruined. On the other hand, if God was the Creator of my meaning and purpose, hadn't I already made a mess of His plans for me as well? This new way of thinking — to which I was being exposed — had me questioning everything and led me to a futile state of mind that lasted for months.

I eventually landed in a campus Bible study that a good friend had urged me to attend. There I heard words that resonated with my deep need for answers, reminding me of Scripture I had heard in Sunday School as a young child. I began to see a way out of the darkness into which I had fallen. The speaker's words pointed my thoughts to someone bigger than me, with a story more awe-inspiring than my own. As I sat on the floor with my back up against the wall, I prayed that learning more about this God of the Bible would end the misery I was experiencing. For the first time in months, I began to feel hopeful. The seeds of truth — sown into my heart as a child — were about to sprout and grow.

I still remember kneeling by my dorm room bed a few weeks later, weeping with joy. For months, I had been despondent. Suddenly, as the truth of the Gospel opened the eyes of my heart, my tears turned into tears of relief. It wasn't too late! Jesus loved me despite my mistakes and failures. I literally felt His face shine on me and His arms hold me tight. There in this secular college setting, Jesus became real to me, and I drank in His peace. Immediately, the heaviness that had engulfed me dissipated. It was a life-changing moment after which the lies I was required to study in the Psychology department no longer influenced me. Jesus met me that evening in my dorm room, and I have trusted my life to Him ever since.

It's the light of Jesus that dissipates darkness. And it's His love story with humanity that will capture the hearts of our children today. In their sorrow, His comfort will be more poignant. In their loneliness, His presence will be more soothing. In their failure, His encouragement will be a welcome relief. He is the Good News! He is our living hope!

Called to Know God

As Christian educators and parents, we are forming young souls by helping them gain a true knowledge of God so that they will grow to love Him, want to imitate Him and become more like Him. We want them to discover a world with God-given order and intrinsic meaning and reconcile to it rather than believe they can create their identity and purpose.

With today's full-frontal attack on the Church and on the validity of the Bible, it's easy to get disoriented. In this confusing, information-rich-noisy culture, our source to know God and His wisdom must be His Word. Not Google. Not social media. We must hold up the entirety and purity of the Bible to our children as the key to life. Believing in God requires that we believe His Word. All of it.

In his letter written from prison — as he anticipated death, Paul wrote to Timothy, *"Avoid the irreverent babble and contradictions of what is falsely called 'knowledge,' for by professing it some have swerved from the faith"* (1 Timothy 6:20-21). This warning is as relevant today as it was in 65 AD.

Also from prison, knowing he too would soon be executed, Peter reminded believers that *"His divine power has granted to us all things that pertain to life and godliness, through the knowledge of him"* (2 Peter 1:3). His final words in 2 Peter 3:18 were an exhortation to *"grow in the grace and knowledge of our Lord and Savior Jesus Christ."*

Our identity, our purpose, our very meaning in life flow out of knowing and loving the Triune God. This requires a firm foundation about His existence and who He is. Knowing God is more than an intellectual pursuit, however. Our children need to know Him personally as:

- A Father who loves them.

- A merciful God whose heart remains tender despite the hardness of our hearts.

- A trustworthy Savior whose nature never changes.

- A compassionate Shepherd who finds them even when they stray.

- A faithful Friend who is always with them.

- A gracious Helper who guides them into Truth.

Created in His Image

Every individual, male, female — regardless of skin color, regardless of imperfections — is *Imago Dei* — created in the image of God. This image is a part of mankind. Regardless of sin, it remains in each one of us as a yearning that cannot be gratified in other ways — although we try.

> *"The yearning to know what cannot be known, to comprehend the incomprehensible, to touch and taste the unapproachable, arises from the image of God in the nature of man. Deep calleth unto deep, and though polluted and landlocked by the mighty disaster theologians call the Fall, the soul senses its origin and longs to return to its source."*[7]

— A. W. Tozer

What does it mean to be *Imago Dei*? To be clear, it does not mean any person is like God. He is incomprehensible. Far beyond our imaginations. *Imago Dei* is a mysterious concept that I struggle to wrap my mind around; yet I find it remarkably transformative. As *Imago Dei*, we were created to become reflections of His character — to be His representatives to a lost and hurting world around us. *Imago Dei* is about the essence of our manhood or womanhood as defined by our Creator. It encompasses the mental, emotional and spiritual components of our lives. The clearer we see God, the more we choose to become His and reflect His image by our love for and unity with others.

God formed us and knit us intricately together — intentionally for the days He established beforehand for us — even before we were born. (Psalm 139:13-15) When our students embrace this truth, they grow confident in God's design and plan for them. As they see themselves as *Imago Dei*, their identity is clarified because they come to understand that they are uniquely made for Him and His glory. Confusion about identity dissipates because anyone who knows who God created them to become will not want to be anyone else. The Bible speaks clearly about *Imago Dei*:

- Genesis 1:26-27 — Let us make man in our image.
- Genesis 5:1-2 — When God created man, He made man in the likeness of God — male and female He created them.
- Romans 8:29 — We are to be conformed to the image of His Son.
- 2 Corinthians 3:18 — We are being transformed into His image.
- Colossians 3:10 — We are to put on the new self, which is being renewed in knowledge after the image of the Creator.
- James 3:9 — We are made in the likeness of God.
- 1 John 3:2 — We will be like Him.

Imago Dei defines not only our identity but our purpose. Dane Orlund in *Gentle and Lowly* said it like this: "*We are pieces of art, designed to be beautiful and thus draw attention to our artist. We are simply made for nothing else. When we live to glorify God, we step into the only truly humanizing way of living."* [10]

Knowing God and seeing ourselves as *Imago Dei* change everything about our human relationships because they change the way we see each other. When I choose to see the imprint of God's image in my children and grandchildren, I can look past poor choices and annoyances and see them as image-bearers in the process of growing and changing.

Called to a New Identity

I am not merely saved by Jesus, but He calls me to a new self: I am to *"put off your old self, which belongs to your former manner of life and is corrupt through deceitful desires, and put on the new self, created after the likeness of God in true righteousness and holiness"* (Ephesians 4:22, 24). When my old self gets out of the way, I better understand what it means to cease resisting and have Jesus be the Lord of my life. Those things about me that destroy life — my angry words or lack of regard for others — are replaced by Christlike virtues such as forgiveness and compassion. The Apostle Paul proclaimed, *"It is no longer I who live, but Christ who lives in me"* (Galatians 2:20).

But my old self tries to persist — reinforced by false labels placed on me by others as well as ones I have pasted on myself. My parents often called me impatient as a child. I grew up thinking impatience was a part of my nature that could not be changed. I certainly behaved as if this were true. I was deeply convicted, however, once I realized that patience is included in the fruit of the Spirit. Ouch! While I have grown much more patient over the years, I still struggle at times and must remind myself that my identity in Christ includes being patient with others.

Another label gained in childhood was that I lacked worth. My parents certainly had many redeeming qualities; but like all of us, they also had blind spots. They did not recognize the importance of investing time in getting to know and understand their five children. We rarely talked with our parents — except about our chores. I grew up feeling like I did not matter to them — except for how I could help them. This label caused me a lot of heartache over the years and unnecessary striving to try to gain worth in the eyes of others. As I learned to find my worth in Jesus, this label has faded. It's still visible at times, but it no longer defines me as it did in previous years.

What kinds of labels are your children sticking onto themselves? Labels are both inferred and self-inflicted. False labels will cause them to live out of their labels and hold them back from becoming who God has called them to be. Children readily apply debilitating labels to themselves such as "*I will never measure up*" or "*I am difficult*" or "*I am unlovable.*" These labels lead to poor choices. The label "*I am not good at math*" causes children to give minimal effort in math class because "*why try hard when it won't make a difference anyway?*" When we allow false labels to define us, we wind up behaving in false ways contrary to who God calls us to be.

What are the labels God places on His children? According to Ephesians 1:3-7, we are blessed "*with every spiritual blessing in the heavenly places*" (v. 3). We are chosen. Holy and blameless. Adopted by God. Loved. Redeemed. Forgiven. These are our God-given identity labels. This is the new self we are to put on, "*which is being renewed in knowledge after the image of its creator*" (Colossians 3:10). Our culture needs us to live from this renewed place. So do our children! We are to put on compassionate, kind, forgiving hearts and love, which unifies us together. (Colossians 3:12-14) Loving God and loving others. That's what we are called to do. When our lives are built upon the foundation of God's love and we choose to abide there, His love breaks through our lives and flows to others. "*By this all people will know that you are my disciples, if you have love for one another*" (John 13:35).

I recently received this testimony from a parent of two children and a highly regarded teacher at Veritas Academy. Her testimony paints a beautiful picture of a mom who is learning to walk in this new identity:

I know these things: Teaching my kids at home is hard; it can be crazy hard; but God is so good and faithful. I have sweet, quiet time with the Lord as I pour over His Word and listen to what He is telling me. These sweet times have increased in regularity as my children have gotten older and more independent. I went from barely having enough time to use the bathroom by myself to modeling what quiet time with the Lord looks like for my preteen children. The years really do go by quickly. This model of education has allowed me more time to grow relationally with my kids and husband. I'm rearing kids that I want to be around! As soon as I stopped trying to rely on my own strength and chasing after the approval of man in so many ways, I was able to grow closer to both God and my family. I am now able to trust that God loves my kids more than I ever could. My goal is that they know and love Him fully. Parenting from this perspective minimized my fears and temptation to compare them to others. My pastor once said, "So you don't think you can handle that situation, huh? Great. Now God can get to work!" I've had high highs and low lows, but they have all brought me to where I am today... seeking God with everything I am and relying on His strength instead of my own. I can't help but feel frustrated that it has taken me so long to experience the joy that comes from letting Him do the hard work in my life. I love the margin this model has created for my family, and I would do it all over again if I had to start over!

Called to His Strength and Not Our Own

We all have a deep need to be made right with God; and until we understand that the Way is Jesus, we will try all sorts of ways to "right" ourselves. Undoubtedly, spiritual disciplines are important for spiritual growth. Bible reading. Prayer. Journaling. Meditating on His Word. These practices have certainly grown my faith and changed me — but in and of themselves, they aren't enough to transform my heart. Making spiritual practices come alive certainly leads to transformation, but they are not the end goal. Knowing Jesus is — and only He can change my heart. Dallas Willard said, "*Grace is not opposed to effort; it is opposed to earning. Earning is an attitude. Effort is an action.* "[12] We can't grow Christlike character without Jesus, but neither will He choose to change a passive heart. Our obedient actions are required in transformation. As Jesus cleans us on the inside (Matthew 23:26), our outsides begin to transform, changing our desires from what we want to do into what we ought to do.

There is a tendency, however, in Christian schools and homes to inadvertently give the message to students that their obedience is what brings about and strengthens the love of God. (Another false label.) Obedience is undoubtedly important; but when students think they leverage Christ's favor and love by their performance and behavior, they make the Gospel about themselves. When their faith morphs into a list of what to do and what to abstain from, they are in danger of becoming "whitewashed tombs" — beautiful on the outside but dead on the inside. They learn how to look saved without being saved. What an anxious way to grow up! For some, it leads to perfectionism, which results in failure because perfection is unattainable. For others, it leads to giving up because the reality that they are not good enough sinks in. In their place, anger and rebellion easily take root.

Cole (name changed) was known as a stellar basketball player. Only one month into the season, the coach invited him to play with the varsity team; and he soon was labeled as the up-and-coming star in the freshman class. Then it happened. During a simple drill at practice, he stepped wrong, fell; and the player behind him crashed down onto him. The result was a broken ankle — one that required surgery and a long recovery. Now Cole was unable to live up to the label that had been placed on him, and he grew deeply discouraged. When a person's identity is formed around what they do well — whether it is academic, athletic, musical or social, such an identify can collapse. Naming our children by their identity as children of God will never fade, however. We don't achieve our Christian identity by our performance. It's a gift we freely receive.

I recently asked a mother of four Veritas graduates to share what her journey has been like as she battled a bent towards perfectionism. She now understands that unhealthy perfectionism, at its core, is an identity issue — one that can demolish one's potential to flourish and live abundant lives. Here's her story:

> *"There should be an app that shows you how many wadded up and discarded pieces of paper you would be using if you were doing a writing assignment on actual paper instead of on a digital platform. It would make us perfectionists feel so good about the forests we are saving. My dear friend and mentor asked me — quite a while ago — to write about being an imperfect parent who struggles with perfectionism. As she put it, "No one can write as well about being an imperfect parent as you can!" Which can be taken a few different ways .... But she's right. As if to prove her point, the past 12 (I counted the deleted drafts) that I've written about this subject — to satisfy her request — have all been deemed too imperfect to submit.*
>
> *And therein lies the rub of a perfectionist, yes? I also — just now — deleted the phrase "I am a perfectionist" because that's an identity statement. I'm working and praying hard these days to make sure that the identity statements I make are true, meaning that they line up with the Word of God. So here's the new statement: "I struggle with perfectionism." That's true. Truer than I would like it to be. Even still.*
>
> *A few years ago, my sister was helping me move out of my house. We were pulling all of my small appliances out of my kitchen cabinets and setting them on the counters to get them ready to be wrapped and boxed up for the transition. The yogurt maker. The waffle maker. The sausage maker*

(attachment). The bread maker. The pizza maker. Etc. When the cabinets were emptied, she looked around at all of them and said, "Did any of these make you the perfect mom that you were obviously trying so hard to be?" Ouch. Maybe if I'd actually used half of them ....

Be perfect, therefore, as your Heavenly Father is perfect. These words — read out of Matthew 5:48 — always stuck in my soul. If there was ever a woman who was NOT perfect — it was I (me?) See?

Perfectionism is defined as a continual striving for flaw-lessness and perfection. It is accompanied by critical self-evaluations and concerns regarding others' evaluations.

However, definitions don't always equal reality. They're definitions. The reality is that perfection means ... Exhaustion. Defeat. Insecurity. Fear. Anxiety. Burnout. Paralysis. Depression.

But the real reality — the worst reality — is that perfectionism is — idolatry. It is putting yourself in place of God. It is putting your standards in place of God's standards. It is also putting your own efforts in place of Christ's work on the cross that makes us perfect.

Perfectionism is — at its core — an identity issue. And so that's where we need to resist it. Attack it. Demolish it. Because — if we don't — it will continually resist our ability to be who God created us to be, attack the identity that God created us to have and demolish our potential to flourish and live abundant lives. No, we are not perfect. We will never be. We were never meant to be. Christ is so that we don't have to be. That truth needs to sink so deep into our hearts, minds and souls that they replace any and all of our perfectionist feelings, thoughts and actions.

Here's the good news: We are not enough, and that is OK. It's more than OK — it's really, really good news! The pathway to becoming all that God calls me to be is embracing the truth that, apart from Christ, I am not enough. But He is enough on my behalf. He is the Vine, and I am a branch. John Piper said, "*The Imago Dei is not a quality possessed by man; it is a condition in which man lives, a condition that is both established and maintained by the Creator.*"[13] What could happen in their lives if our boys and girls got this right? What would their lives look like if they sought regeneration and not self-affirmation? What if they let go of the dictates of their hearts and instead walked in the labels placed on every individual who receives Christ as their Lord and Savior?

Before I understood this truth personally, my life was defined by striving to be the best I could be. Striving to please others. Striving for affirmation. Striving to be productive and valued. Victory came when I finally quit striving and found soul rest in Jesus instead. It's in this place that my efforts turn fruitful. Whenever I step back into relying mostly on my efforts — and I still do from time to time, a heaviness of spirit encompasses me. Thankfully, Jesus always welcomes me back into His presence, where once again, the striving ceases. I can live and work out of a place of joy — regardless of circumstances.

In Jeremiah 17:5-8, we find a stark contrast between the person who trusts in himself and makes flesh his strength and the person who trusts in the Lord — whose trust *is* the Lord. The former is like a shrub in the desert who dwells in parched places and will see no good come. The latter is like a tree planted by water that sends out its roots by the stream and does not fear when heat comes or grows anxious because its leaves remain green and it does not cease to bear fruit. Despite what we see and hear happening around us, our families can flourish and bear fruit when we put our confidence in Christ and abide closely with Him in this journey of life.

Called to HOPE

When I hope, I choose to believe that God's redemption and goodness remain — regardless of the threats that come against me or the circumstances in which I find myself. Even when disappointment happens and discouragement sets in, God's sovereign nature assures me that He is for my ultimate good and remains at the center of everything that happens. Everything! The Apostle Paul referred to God as the God of hope in Romans 15:13 — who fills us *"with all joy and peace in believing, so that by the power of the Holy Spirit you may abound in hope."* We are not promised an easy life — free of trials. At some point, in fact, we all will likely face trials of various kinds. We are promised, however, that He will be with us in our pain, in our sorrow, in our joys and triumphs, in our everything. Emmanuel. God is with us! God's promises are gifts received by faith and not by merit. Jesus has given us His very life; and as we learn to rely on the Holy Spirit within us. His love, His peace and His hope become a consistent reality. *"We have this as a sure and steadfast anchor of the soul"* — this is our hope! (Hebrews 6:19)

Life is about choices. Hope is a choice. Remaining hopeful is about releasing my grip on control; letting go of my plans, feelings and desires and laying them all down to the omnipotent will of God — regardless of what that means. In this place, anxiety is kept at bay. Life takes on a bearable weight because I am yoked with God who created me, leads me and walks with me.

In *Gentle and Lowly,* Dane Orlund describes two approaches for how to live as a Christian:

I can live for the heart of Christ or from it.

I can live for the smile of God or from it.

I can live for a new identity as a child of God or from it.

I can live for union with Christ or from it.[11]

FOR or FROM: a huge difference. Our children live anxious lives when they try to live *for* God's approval. Rather than a place of flourishing, it's a place of discouragement instead. On the other hand, when they live instead *from* God's approval — granted to them unconditionally by Jesus and His sacrifice on the cross, they will flourish. They can place their hope in Him with confidence because He will equip them for what He calls them to.

FIVE PRACTICAL APPLICATIONS

ONE: Strengthen your own apologetics

Even the very existence of God is being hotly debated today, and our children need to be prepared to engage in these conversations — both knowledgeably and compassionately. While their influence will rise out of engaging conversations that are about winning people and not just winning arguments, they will need a foundation from which to engage in these conversations. They need to know why they believe what they believe. We can help them justify their faith by both facts and personal experiences. I am no theologian, but I know that faith in God is not just an emotional experience but also a rational one. My faith strengthens when I consider how God's truths stand the test of rationality.

We must prepare them for a world in which a progressive Christian movement seeks to deconstruct Biblical truth and question essential components of faith to make it palatable to current thought. Discuss these views with your children regularly. There is no new Gospel. Period. Ensure that your children are learning unchanging truths based on historical Christianity and not growing seeds of doubt by way of false — but popular — ideas. Jesus said that *"whoever causes one of these little ones who believe in me to sin, it would be better for him to have a great millstone fastened around his neck and to be drowned in the depth of the sea"* (Matthew 18:6).

The Bible is the story of God's loving relationship with humanity, an overarching narrative that relates to our very being. God's Word has demonstrated transformative power over the ages; and it will change your life and that of your kids, too! Historical records support the authenticity and historical accuracy of His Word — a cohesive story formed by 40 authors over two continents during a period of 1,500 years. With confidence, you can view your experience via the lens of the Bible rather than trying to view the Bible through the lens of your experiences.

Many resources exist for individuals like me, who don't have a theological background. Older classics — like *Knowing God* by J. I. Packer and *The Knowledge of the Holy* by A. W. Tozer — deepened my knowledge of God. Here are a few, newer sources that I have found to be helpful in this journey:

- *A Practical Guide to Culture*[14] by John Stonestreet and Brett Kunkle
- *Cold Case Christianity*[15] by J. Warner Wallace
- *Another Gospel?*[16] by Alisa Childers

TWO: Teach your children who the true HERO is

Bradley (name changed) was desperate to make a name for himself. Academics had been a struggle. Several injuries sidelined him from sports, so he decided to give music a try. His aim was to become famous — regardless of a lack of experience, and this quest became an obsession that eventually led him to make some horrific choices. He eventually landed in jail. Now he is struggling to work his way out of a host of problems he created for himself when this desire for fame became an unquenchable obsession.

Bradley is not alone. In recent years, fame has become the top aim for many young people — not faith, not family or friendship but personal fame. Kids want to be known, to be the heroes of their stories, to do something grand that gets attention. Some are even willing to make seriously dumb choices like establishing a social media presence that can cost them dearly in the future. We all have a deep need to matter somehow, to be known; but messages like "you can be anything you want to be" or "do anything you want to do" often end in despair.

Of course, we want our children to set high goals for themselves and achieve these goals. We want to see them work hard in the classroom, out on the sports field, on the dance floor and with any activity in which they choose to participate; so they will be prepared to enter the adult world with strong skills and abilities. Their moral formation must include a strong work ethic, which sets them up to contribute meaningfully to society. However, the most important things happen within the context of ordinary life where their character is formed. Who they are at home matters more than the fame they crave outside the home. Each team on which they participate will have one MVP. Every race has one winner. A graduating class will have a valedictorian. Olympic sports have one gold medalist. A single team becomes the March Madness champion. Not everyone will win. But everyone can be successful in their day in and day out rhythm of life. Each child can find success and fulfillment, and their lives will take on lasting meaning when they walk as His children and give God the glory for being their HERO in the process.

Tozer stated, *"The widest thing in the universe is not space; it is the potential capacity of the human heart. Being made in the image of God, it is capable of almost unlimited extension in all directions. And one of the world's greatest tragedies is that we allow our hearts to shrink until there is room in them for little besides ourselves."*[8]

We certainly want our children to reach their full potential, which can be fulfilled only as they understand their identity as children of God. Then out of that shared identity with other believers, they can begin to embrace their unique personhood. Out of a deep need for recognition, Bradley looks to what he thinks his peers value. Desiring to gain worldly attention and favor, he set out to become a famous singer-songwriter but without the talent, expertise or work ethic to accomplish this aim. Trying to become a version of someone else, he has lost sight entirely of his unique strengths and identity. As I write, he is still floundering. I pray that he will find his way out of the well of confusion into which he has fallen by looking up at God who made him and desires to save Bradley from himself. I pray that someday he will see Jesus as his Hero rather than trying to become a hero himself.

THREE: Teach your children to treat
every person with dignity and respect

This place is where we can agree with loud voices in culture. We are all equal in value and dignity. John Piper said, *"As God's image bearers, every single human being, no matter how much the image of God is marred by sin, or illness, or weakness, or age, must be treated with dignity and respect."*[15] We treat each other with dignity and respect when we listen, seek to understand and consider what others need — even those with whom we don't agree. We can respond to others compassionately without compromising what we believe and, in the process, model this to our kids. How we treat each other is the best teacher! Respond to your children respectfully and thoughtfully. Smile at them whenever possible. Greet them enthusiastically. Let them overhear you talking about how much you love and value them. In doing so, you are establishing in them the tools to treat others with dignity and respect as well.

Look for the *Imago Dei* in your children. Look for specks of brilliance beneath the dirt that can be easier to spot. Recognize each child's unique strengths, which may even come out of their weaknesses. As mentioned earlier, your strong-willed little ones are destined for leadership. Your argumentative son may become an apologist. Your impulsive daughter may become a creative artist or writer. Choose to focus on their strengths more than their weaknesses.

FOUR: Parent the child you have and
avoid the comparison trap

Each of your children is born with gifts and strengths that will equip them to run in the lane God has chosen for them. As Dr. Kathy Koch says,

"Each child is created on purpose, with purpose, for purpose." I am amazed at how uniquely different each of my grandkids are. Likewise, each child of yours is a blend of both strengths and weaknesses that you can help them identify. Then you can form a plan by which to both grow their strengths and address their weaknesses — which if left undealt with — can block them from growing and flourishing.

My granddaughters, Hadassah and Greta, invest a lot of time into Irish dance — something at which they are very good. However, both have been reluctant to try other activities — worried they may not be as successful in them. Yet their parents know they will grow more resilient by investing time in both their areas of strengths and weaknesses. Therefore, both girls currently are playing on our school's soccer teams — not because they chose to but because their parents insisted. What I assumed would be a difficult experience is turning out to be a lot of fun for each of them. They are learning new skills without the expectation to be very good. And they love the team experience! At an older age, they will be allowed to narrow their focus to those things they love best.

Joey, Kate and Will are my oldest daughter's children. Even though they always have been reared in the same home, they are vastly different from each other. Things come easy for Joey, but he would benefit from putting in greater effort and engaging wholeheartedly. He is organized, efficient and tidy; but he can be somewhat risk averse, hesitating to try challenging things. His sister Kate works hard and willingly tries anything — but she is ineffective with time and easily gets lost in a daydream world. Her room often looks like a tornado blew through it. Their younger brother Will is wholeheartedly engaged in absolutely everything he does, but he needs to learn how to slow down and ponder what he is doing. He can be the tornado that leaves a trail of destruction behind him. They each need to be parented uniquely in a manner that addresses their strengths and flaws personally.

Just like Joey, Kate and Will, God created each of your children to run their race, and He will equip them to do so. They will be weighed down, however, when they step out of their lane. Your introverted child will not engage socially like your extrovert. Your artistic child may thrive in art and music class but be unmotivated on the soccer field. They will find little joy or grace outside of God's chosen plan for them. That's why we need to stop looking around and comparing our kids or ourselves with others.

A clear scheme of the enemy is the comparison trap, but comparison is a joy killer. When we compare ourselves to others, hope, vision and joy die. When our children feel jealous or envious of others, it may reflect that they find it hard to fit into the lane God has chosen for them. It's so easy to have feelings of inadequacy — even in the midst of success — to focus on what goes wrong instead of all that goes right! We experience the fullness of joy from the Lord, however, when we live surrendered lives, according to His plans for us. Jesus said, *"The thief comes only to steal and kill and destroy. I came that they may have life and have it abundantly"* (John 10:10). So embrace and equip the kids you have — even if they don't fit the mold of who you want them to be. They will be satisfied with their strengths and giftings when you are.

FIVE: Respond wisely to the issues of today

Rearing kids in today's culture can feel frightening. Today's issues are far different than they were a mere decade ago; so I asked my son, Troy Schuknecht, to address what he views as the major challenges that influence our children away from what matters most in life. Troy has served as the administrator of our upper school at Veritas Academy since 2008, and he is the father of four children — his eldest being born in 2008 as well. He works closely with students and their parents, and he considers digital entertainment and the modern progressive view of humanity to be the major issues faced by families today. Here's what he had to say:

There is nothing with greater potential to undermine discipleship with our kids than digital entertainment. While gaming and binging punchy, quick videos are rewiring brains, social media is shifting the allegiance of hearts. Most forms of digital entertainment mold a child into a student who struggles to pay attention, whose brain cannot process complex texts and who has lost curiosity. Social media compounds this. Jeremiah 17:9 reminds us that all humans have a deceitful heart. The human experience is one of thinking and feeling things that aren't true. A steady diet of Scripture, prayer and time spent listening to God is our only hope to straighten out our crooked hearts. Modern kids spend far less time with spiritual disciplines and far more time on digital entertainment that consistently reinforces as valid the thoughts and feelings of their hearts. In my conversations with crying parents over such challenges, they usually describe a screen addiction and countless hours each day spent on social media and video streaming applications.

There is no easy solution. A good starting place, however, is to diligently limit screens and create screen-free times for everyone. Mealtime. Car rides together as a family. Personal quiet times. A reasonable hour when all screens are shut down for the night. Consider how much free time your children have which, all too often, morphs into screen time. All children need reasonable amounts of activities, such as sports or music or art, during which screens have no place. Put parental controls on your children's phones and screens. Know what they are doing in the digital world. Digital technology will severely undermine your influence, so have a plan to reduce this and give your children the opportunity to become all God has called them to be.

The second issue of our day is the culture's vision of humanity. A vision where the self reigns. Where what we feel is what is real. Where living authentically in light of who you feel you are is not only where freedom is found but is brave. Courage is viewed as not succumbing to the pressure of norms but instead being true to yourself. On the contrary, aligning oneself to absolute truth is a sign of weakness.

Since this is the prevailing thinking and a message reinforced everywhere, we should not be surprised by what we see in youth today. Hookup culture. Casual sexual encounters. Substance abuse. Addiction to pornography. The LGBTQ+ movement. How can parents respond to all this? Start by ensuring that no sin is too taboo to talk about, to gain freedom from and forgiveness over. Make your home a safe place to work through sin and get past it. Keep in mind that all sins are damaging, offensive to God and something to be battled against. Therefore, approach your child with humility. We are all sinners in need of grace.

Don't identify your children by their sins. None of us wants to be identified by our worst moments, so we must fight to ensure that our children are not reduced down to theirs. Don't respond in fear when your child admits a sin. It means he or she feels safe enough with you to share. Be known more for what you are for than what you are against. Model a counter-cultural God-centeredness by infusing your days with intentional opportunities to gain a bigger view of God and a smaller view of self.

Whatever you or your child is currently facing is not too large for our God, so take a deep breath and enjoy the perfect peace He promises. A peace that surpasses comprehension is promised to you if you will cast your anxiety upon Him.

CHAPTER TWO

Called to Be Disciple-Makers

"Making disciples of Jesus is the overflow of the delight in being disciples of Jesus."[17]
— David Platt *Follow Me: A Call to Die. A Call to Live.*

When Jesus commissioned His 11 to go and make disciples, He told them to teach their disciples to observe all that Jesus had commanded them. (Matthew 28:20) Making disciples starts with our children by training and instructing them in the discipline and instruction of Jesus – in how He lived His life. (Ephesians 6:4) These spiritual practices are God-ordained means by which our lives are transformed over time. They form good habits through which we naturally begin to express the fruit of His Spirit and slowly begin to become more like Him.

I ran track in high school; and because I was not very fast, I chose the longer distances. Being competitive, I wanted to win; but trying to win without sufficient training did not work. Regardless of how badly I wanted to run well — because I was a novice, I faltered and ran out of steam. It took consistent training and practice — over time — to finish a long race well. In several Scriptures, our spiritual walks are described as races. Hebrews 12:1 instructs us to *"run with endurance the race that is set before us."* 1 Corinthians instructs us to not run aimlessly but with discipline in order to gain an imperishable wreath. Just as in physical races, our spiritual walks require training and disciplined practice to adopt the practices of Jesus as our own. Without Him, our lives will not transform; yet transformation requires our obedient efforts.

Making disciples in our homes begins with being disciples of Jesus ourselves. What does it look like to follow Jesus? Perhaps you are blessed with a child who works hard, behaves, treats others respectfully and even willingly goes to church with you. These actions may lead you to believe that he or she is following Jesus; yet this may not necessarily be the case. How does one define a disciple of Jesus? To help answer this question, I turn to pastor Dr. John Turner, a friend and mentor, who serves as a UMSI Ministry Advisor. He is the author of the inspirational book, *Character-Driven College Preparation*. Dr. Turner's heart is to see fruitful disciples come out of our schools who impact the next generation, which is the vision that drives our schools. The following is based on what Dr. Turner shared:

To understand how Jesus defines a disciple, we need only to look at the words of the Master Himself:

"... 'If anyone would come after me, let him deny himself and take up his cross daily and follow me'" (Luke 9:23).

1. *"... 'If you abide in my word, you are truly my disciples'"* (John 8:31).

2. *"And he told them a parable to the effect that they ought always to pray and not lose heart"* (Luke 18:1).

3. *"By this all people will know that you are my disciples, if you have love for one another"* (John 13:35).

4. *"... 'and you will be my witnesses in Jerusalem and in all Judea and Samaria, and to the end of the earth'"* (Acts 1:8).

5. *"The greatest among you shall be your servant"* (Matthew 23:11).

Dr. Turner condensed these verses into a cohesive picture, saying, "*The picture Jesus draws is a follower who intentionally nurtures a daily sacrificial walk with Christ, feeds constantly on God's Word, prays with faith and fervor, loves as Jesus loves, bears witness of Jesus everywhere, and does it all with an unselfish servant's heart."* [18] Becoming a follower of Jesus is a lifelong journey. When our children receive Jesus into their hearts as their Lord and Savior, they have merely stepped out of the gate onto this path. Admittedly, upon first reading Dr. Turner's description, I began to think of how often I fall short of this standard. Then I turned my thoughts instead to how far along this journey the Lord already has led me. I still have a long way to go; but at least, I am out of the gate and running!

Discipleship is a way of life in which we are to walk as we guide our children to live the lives that God has designed for them. I am inspired by the words of Eugene H. Peterson, author of *The Message: The Bible in Contemporary Language,* who wrote, *"Christian discipleship is a decision to walk in his ways, steadily and firmly, and then finding that the way integrates all our interests, passions, and gifts, our human needs and eternal aspirations. It is the way of life we were created for."* [21]

Helping children gain a solid academic foundation — one that is immersed in the Biblical worldview — is very important; yet the highest role God places on parents is that of being disciple-makers in their homes. Dr. Turner wisely states, *"Schools cannot make the disciples described above en masse. But moms and dads can make them at home."* [19] This is God's design! The role of University-Model® Schools is to journey with parents so that they don't feel alone, overwhelmed or unsupported as they walk along the challenging road of discipling children to mature faith. Elisabeth Elliot, a favorite author of mine, wrote, *"God gives to fallible parents this little boy or girl, who will certainly prove to be far from perfect, to love and train and teach, to bring up, in the 'nurture and admonition,' the training and instruction, of the Lord. It's a serious assignment. There is no higher calling."*

Perhaps you feel discouraged or lost in this challenging journey of walking as disciple-makers for your children. You are not the only parent who feels this way. I have met with countless moms and dads, who consider themselves inadequate to disciple their children. Others disqualify themselves due to past mistakes. As a result, they hand this role off to someone else. Other parents expect way too much of themselves, then feel like failures when their kids struggle. I certainly felt discouraged and inadequate as a young parent. I assumed that I was responsible to transform my children's hearts — a burden that exhausted me. But I was holding onto a responsibility that was not mine to carry. Only God can do the work in our children's hearts. I can only be faithful to carry out my role. God loves our children even more than we do, and He will equip you to disciple the very children He intentionally placed in your care.

So what is our role as disciple-makers? Listed next are suggested practices to instill in your homes; but before contemplating these ideas, set your expectations realistically. If these practices currently are not a reality for you, tackle them one at a time. These practices form a foundation for authentic discipleship; but it's a journey that takes place over time — with conversations that should span years. Discipleship is more a lifestyle than a series of events. Here are some ideas that can turn discipleship into a way of life in your family.

Practice 1 — Study and apply God's Word to your life as you teach your children to do the same.

Your children are more likely to become who they think you are rather than what they hear you say. Therefore, discipling your children begins with steadfastly seeking Him yourself. Do your children see you studying God's Word? Do you share with them how you are applying His Word to your life? Do they know where your strength comes from?

Growing as a disciple of Jesus rests primarily in one's abiding — and not in one's striving. Regardless of how hard we try, we cannot bear fruit for the Kingdom of God apart from abiding in Christ. I spent years striving to follow Jesus in my strength, and it left me feeling utterly desolate and broken. Relief began to flood my soul when I focused instead on the truth in these words of Jesus:

- *"Whoever abides in me and I in him, he it is that bears much fruit, for apart from me you can do nothing"* (John 15:5).

- *"But the Helper, the Holy Spirit, whom the Father will send in my name, he will teach you all things and bring to your remembrance all that I have said to you"* (John 14:26).

Knowing that Jesus left us with the Helper makes studying His Word come alive in inspiring ways. As we read His Word, the Holy Spirit guides us into all truth. (John 16:13) In addition, prayer becomes intimate and life-giving, with the burdens of life seeming lighter to bear. As followers, we have the wonderful gift of the Holy Spirit who empowers and guides us to walk as Christ's Ambassadors. Your kids need to see you walking in this manner so that they too will be irresistibly drawn to Him — out of desire and not out of duty.

Practice 2 — Conduct daily small-group God-times as a family.

"You shall teach them diligently to your children, and shall talk of them when you sit in your house, and when you walk by the way, and when you lie down, and when you rise" (Deuteronomy 6:7). This directive to parents is a call to integrate what God commands of us into our daily interactions with our children — to participate in their spiritual lives regularly and actively, impressing God's commandments upon their hearts through conversation, study and prayer.

For most parents, it's not a matter of wanting to. Rather it's a matter of finding the time. Many of the most effective God-times can happen spontaneously, however, in response to what is going on at the moment.

On Thursdays, three of the grandchildren who come to my home for their school day are strong-willed boys. I have been teaching them what it means to be loving, using 1 Corinthians 13 as the source. Each week I ask them to consider how they are applying love *"does not insist on its own way"* (v.5) as they play and work together. Moments like these make Scripture come alive when I point them to how they can apply God's truth to what they are experiencing. Knowledge then moves to understanding, and understanding is what leads to heart change. I love how they are learning to consider each other, considering God's Word.

In addition, mealtimes provide a great setting for the family to discuss God's Word in a relaxed fashion. Car rides do as well — if everyone puts their phones away! Finding time can be challenging, but look for ways to bring in these God-times — even if it is only a few minutes at a time.

Having time for yourself to study God's Word can be difficult, especially when your children are young. I loved how my oldest daughter, Erin, solved this issue. As she read the Bible and journaled her thoughts each morning, she provided her children with journals as well and invited them to sit quietly by her and do the same.

For planned Bible study times with your whole family, here are a few TIPS to consider:

- Maintain a reasonably short time — based on how long your children can remain engaged.
- Maintain a calm, relaxed, warm atmosphere.
- Engage everyone in reading Scripture and praying.
- Have members tell what verses mean and how they can be applied to life.
- Encourage — and make room for — genuine questions.
- Don't be legalistic about these study times or be guilty about missing a time.

Making God a genuine part of your daily life is far more influential than adhering to a strict schedule. Prior to offering up the directive to parents in Deuteronomy 6, Moses told his people, *"love the LORD your God with all your heart and with all your soul and with all your might"* (Deuteronomy 6:5). When loving God is a reality in your life, your children will be far more likely to fall in love with Him and desire to be in His Word as well.

Practice 3 — Pray in faith without losing heart.

A few years back, we took on the challenge — and blessing — of taking care of my mom in her final years as she struggled with Alzheimer's disease. We call her our prayer warrior because — no matter what took place, no matter how large or small an issue — she immediately would call for prayer as her offense and defense. I watched a vibrant prayer life change my mom in beautiful ways. While her mind deteriorated, her intimacy with Jesus did not. In her final years, only prayer and Scripture would calm her anxious thoughts as she dealt with a ravaging disease. *"Jesus"* was the last word she uttered before passing away. God's truth was stored in her heart, and no illness could take that away from her.

I want to leave this same legacy for my children and grandchildren. When I look back on my heritage, I see how prayers offered over the generations have formed a stream of living hope running through the decades. As a young child, I drew inspiration from knowing that my great-grandmother, Sophia, prayed that her daughter (my grandmother) and her future children would be blessed by God with enduring faith. My grandparents, who lived in Finland, prayed fervently for their eight children in the same manner. My prayer-warrior mother finally surrendered her life to Jesus in her 40s. Prayers are not bound by space or time. They are "time released" — free of time restraints; and they live on, impacting lives decades later.

If I am to walk in God's love for me, I must establish a rhythm of prayer in my daily life. The most effective means for me has been to keep prayer journals. I have a large stack of them, which form a record of my prayers and God's answers. Writing down prayers keeps me focused as I pray and helps me to remember what He has done. I pull down these journals from time to time when I need reminders of God's faithfulness in response to my prayers.

Jesus gave us the perfect example of walking and talking with God. He prayed fervently and with reverence. (The Lord's Prayer - Matthew 6:9-13) He prayed with thanksgiving. (Luke 10:21) He prayed that the will of the Father be done. (Matthew 26:39) He encouraged praying with humility. (Luke 18:9-14) He prayed often. Prayer was a critical part of His life. Jesus told us, *"Ask, and it will be given to you"* (Matthew 7:7a). Prayers that call for an answer or a solution to present needs can result in discouragement however when they don't play out as desired. I remember how devastated my youngest daughter and her husband felt when an adoption for which they had planned fell through due to a change of heart by the birth mom after the birth of her child. What they didn't know at the time was that God had reserved a place in their home and hearts for Asa, who was adopted a few months later. God is faithful, sovereign; and He is for our good — but in His timing and in His ways. So as we pray, we also must trust in His divine will and timing.

A vibrant prayer life is how we maintain an intimate relationship with God daily. We praise Him for His faithfulness. We give thanks for His goodness. We lay our requests at His feet, and we also seek His presence and guidance in all that we do. As we do this throughout our days, a peace *"which surpasses all understanding"* falls over us and guards our hearts and minds in Christ Jesus. (Philippians 4:7).

Practice 4 — Nurture healthy, wholesome relationships that show the love of Jesus.

What matters most in life is relational. In fact, our primary identity is relational in nature. A vibrant relationship with God leads to a healthy, content relationship with self. From such a relationship, we can parent our children in confidence and trust and walk in healthy, connected relationships with others.

Life flows into me through my loving attachment to Jesus, who in turn is attached to the Father who commands us to develop loving attachments with others. Close attachments with our children deeply impact their identity and character. It's how they come to know themselves. A strong, lasting relationship with you nurtures their faith, their character and the resilience they need to make it through times when things go wrong. Of course, God CAN accomplish His purposes without parents; but He placed parents into the primary role of discipleship with their children and invited them into this very rewarding work!

Maintaining relational connection is vital not only to maintain our influence but also for the development of virtue and identity. I find this especially important during challenging moments, so I endeavor to remain connected. That is because I know that their identity is formed through close attachments and their character is being refined in relationships of love. On days when I have had to hold the line with a grandchild who is making poor choices, I also take the time — later on — to explain how I love him or her too much to let the poor character go unchecked. I explain how it would be easier to just ignore their misbehavior, but that would not be loving. Then I make sure to affirm them and express belief in who they are becoming. My love matters more during these challenging times than during the smooth times because it is then that I can show them how Jesus loves. These joyful bonds are essential for their growth.

I am even more convinced today that a loving, connected parent-child relationship is invaluable for the transfer of faith and the growth of virtuous character in our children. Influence comes by way of connection — a belief that is substantiated in a book called *The Other Half of Church*. The authors, Jim Wilder and Michel Henricks, paint a compelling picture —

based on brain research — about the importance of joyful bonds between parent and children. They claim that attachment is the strongest force in human relationships and that stable, deep connections form the pathway through which identity is formed. [22]

Practice 5 — Communicate the Good News to neighbors and friends.

The term *evangelical* derives from the Greek word *evangelion*, meaning the *Gospel* or the *Good News* of Jesus Christ. Scriptures direct us to:

- Proclaim the Gospel. (Mark 16:15)

- Be prepared to make a defense to anyone who asks you for a reason for the hope that is in you – with gentleness and respect. (1 Peter 3:15)

- Be His witnesses to all. (Acts 1:8)

These commands are for our kids too, who can be the most effective evangelists with their peers. They need to be taught, however, how to share the Gospel effectively. When kids learn to confidently tell others about Jesus, it not only grows their faith; but it also deepens their compassion for others. Therefore, as their parents:

- Teach your kids that the Great Commission isn't just for adults.

- Equip them to respectfully proclaim the Gospel — with a prepared defense — for the hope that is in them.

- Encourage them to see opportunities to share the Good News in the world around them: in their neighborhoods, at school, on their sport teams or at their social events.

Paul charged Timothy to *"do the work of an evangelist"* (2 Timothy 4:5). He told him to patiently preach the Word (2 Timothy 4:2), *"for the time is coming when people will not endure sound teaching, but having itching ears they will accumulate for themselves teachers to suit their own passions, and will turn away from listening to the truth and wander off into myths"* (2 Timothy 4:3-4). These words sound as if they were written for today. We are certainly living in tumultuous times during which God's truth is being attacked. Yet the Gospel is what every heart needs. Jesus is *"the way, and the truth, and the life"* (John 14:6); and He is our *"sure and steadfast anchor of the soul"* (Hebrews 6:19).

Perhaps the best way to teach our kids how to share the Good News is to have them learn from observing us. My mom purchased hundreds of tiny booklets printed with the "Four Spiritual Laws"; and she would pass them out everywhere she went, greeting people with *"Jesus loves you."* Some would reject her, but a few would stop and ask her more — hungry for good news. Many resources are available that teach the basic Gospel message, which would help kids learn how to express the Gospel in simple, clear ways.

Practice 6 — Develop hearts of servanthood.

The teachings of Jesus reflect a life of love and caring for the needy. In the parable of the great banquet, as recorded in Luke 14:13-14, Jesus said, *"… when you give a feast, invite the poor, the crippled, the lame, the blind, and you will be blessed.…"* Jesus cares about the hurting and the needy and so should we. How can your family contribute to the needs of others in your community? In what practical ways can your family serve others together — either in your neighborhood or on mission trips?

How do we teach servant-heartedness to our kids? I believe it begins by establishing expectations for how we are to treat each other within our homes. When my grandkids enter the school day in my home, they know that one rule applies to everything and it's Jesus' golden rule in Matthew 7:12a: *"So whatever you wish that others would do to you, do also to them."* This rule establishes high expectations for treating one another with dignity and respect. I don't like to be interrupted. I want to be listened to and understood. I desire compassionate care when hurt. I need to be forgiven. Therefore, I should treat others in the same manner I desire to be treated. Regularly reminding my grandkids of this standard influences the culture of these school days at home.

School days at home provide an excellent opportunity for siblings to learn how to work together and help each other. Last spring, my sixth-grade granddaughter, Hadassah, helped her second-grade brother and sister with solar system projects. From start to finish, over the course of several weeks, she worked with them in designing, creating and writing about the planets they had chosen to present. Not only did this help her parents, but she grew through the process and so did her brother and sister.

We also teach servant-heartedness by expecting each member of the family to work for the good of the family. From the earliest ages, kids should be participating in household chores. Not only does this work build life skills, but it establishes values that are not just focused on self. Teach your kids to look for opportunities to serve, and guide them to understand what it means to be a servant. Whenever you see your kids spontaneously doing this, make sure to acknowledge their good deeds because to what we pay attention will grow. When this truth is integrated into their lives, they will be enriched and more fulfilled.

Finally, we "wash each other's feet." Jesus told His disciples, *"If I then, your Lord and Teacher, have washed your feet, you also ought to wash one another's feet. For I have given you an example, that you also should do just as I have done to you"* (John 13:14-15). How do we wash each other's feet? By putting ourselves in a vulnerable place for the benefit of another. By humbly and cheerfully doing things for others we don't feel like doing. By encouraging others with life-giving words of hope. Jesus did not come to be served but to serve, and we will be blessed by following His example. (John 13:17)

As stated earlier, these six practices form a foundation upon which authentic discipleship occurs. When moms and dads embrace their

God-given roles as disciple-makers, they find it transforms them as well. I will conclude this chapter with what one parent recently wrote:

> *"While education is the primary focus of our partnership, the personal growth — experienced through the training provided to the parents — has impacted every part of my life. My husband and I chose this model of school for our children to get the best education possible, and they have; but we didn't realize the decision would be so transformative in us as well."*

CHAPTER THREE

Called to Be Deliberate Dads

By Glen Schuknecht

I didn't plan to join my wife Ellen at Veritas Academy. I envisioned retirement for both of us at this point in our lives. Yet God called me to Veritas Academy as well, where I continue to teach mathematics courses and serve on the facilities team. Back when I taught mathematics courses to my kids, I could not have imagined a time when I would be teaching the same courses to my grandkids. Yet it is exactly what I am doing. As a member of the facilities team, I also get to see my grandkids as they play outside or transition from one class to another. Working at Veritas allows me to be a part of something grand that is taking place within families, including my own.

In this chapter, I hope to offer insights regarding intentional ways fathers can serve their wives and children — how we can become dads with deliberate intentions, conscientiously considering the needs of our family members. I look back with gratitude on 47 years of marriage and rearing three great kids; but at the same time, I realize that I should have been more deliberate about discipling their hearts. To be deliberate is to give careful and thorough consideration — to intentionally rear them into disciples of Jesus. As I watch my 11 grandkids grow, I realize how different the times are today and how even more important it has become for fathers to intentionally focus on what matters most. I write this chapter to encourage you to not get to the end of your child-rearing years and wonder "what happened." Character and spiritual formation won't happen by chance but by deliberate, intentional discipleship. And dads — you matter greatly. What you do — day in and day out — within the walls of your home will greatly influence your children. So be deliberate. Make your time count. They will be gone sooner than you think!

The Bull's Eye

We have a small archery range on our property; and at times, our family holds archery contests. To consistently hit the bull's eye requires deliberate effort — practicing the skills and techniques to accurately send the arrow towards the black dot in the middle of the target. Our youngest grandkids are pleased by just hitting the target anywhere; but more often, their arrows fly off into the hillside beyond. Our older grandkids better understand the steps to shooting an arrow. They position their feet and bodies to face the target, raise and draw the arrow back, aim and release. They are more likely to get close to — and even hit — the bull's eye from time to time.

As parents, God grants us an incredible opportunity to mold and shape our children before they go out into the world on their own. This short, opportune season in our lives often can be a major challenge; but thankfully, God extends grace over and over when we fall short. Psalm 127:3-4 says, "… *children are a heritage from the LORD, the fruit of the womb a reward. Like arrows in the hand of a warrior are the children of one's youth.*" Like a warrior, we must intentionally sharpen, shape and care for our arrows. Ruth Schwenk wrote, "*It's about straightening what's crooked. Sanding the rough spots. Sharpening the point. Adjusting the feathers. Dedicating time to target practice. It's making sure this arrow understands its purpose, the reason it will someday be free in flight.*"[23]

What purposes do you desire for your children when they will be free in flight? What do you want them to aim for? The largest outer ring could represent things like good table manners and learning to speak respectfully to others with "yes ma'am/no sir" and "please/thank you." Then the middle rings could represent the skills of learning such as focus on and attention to detail, a work ethic, disciplined lives as well as pragmatic skills that set them on a path towards success in a career field. The bull's eye represents the most important aims, however. The greatest commandment comes to mind — that they learn to love the Lord with all their hearts, souls and minds and love their neighbors as themselves.

At some point, your children will leave the quiver. What are the most important qualities your son or daughter needs to learn from you? And what are your most important roles as their father? Spend some time answering these questions for your family.

What Must I Be Deliberate About?

In 1974, Dr. Vern L. Bengtson launched an empirical study — the longest of its kind — on faith and families. He began by studying 356 families — all interviewed every three months. By 2013, the pool had grown to more than 3,500 family members. Dr. Bengtson put his findings into a book called *Families and Faith: How Religion Is Passed Down Across Generations.* [24] He concluded that parents (and grandparents) have greater influence than they think, that emotional bonds are most important and that particularly important are a father's warmth and affirmation with regard to the passing of faith to the next generation. Let me say that again. Particularly important are a father's warmth and affirmation! Admittedly, I leaned towards believing that my primary role was to run a "tight ship" and be a strict disciplinarian. While holding children to high standards of behavior is very important, Bengtson's research found that doing so — with authoritarian methods — served to diminish faith. His research affirms that we dads and granddads matter. We cannot leave the teaching of faith and values to our wives — even though it often comes more naturally to them. We too must connect emotionally and warmly with our children, and we must expect virtuous standards in loving and thoughtful ways.

A few years ago, I heard a college girl in our church say, *"I know what a great counselor God is. I know He is sovereign, and He gives me peace; but I never knew my own father, so I really struggle to see God as my "Everlasting Father."* As I listened to this young woman talk, I began to wonder how young people, who are estranged from their dads, feel when they hear prayers sent to "our Father in heaven"? This made me reflect on my relationship with my three children. How did my treatment of them impact their view of God? Did they see me as affirming or critical? Did I extend forgiveness when they needed it or further condemnation? Did they feel that they could approach me about anything, or were they more apt to hide their true feelings from me? I remember plenty of good times but also some mistakes. While I can't go back and change the past, my present life includes 11 grandkids who look to me as the patriarch of our family. I long for them to see me as a warm, affirming, virtuous and faith-filled grandfather. I want their view of me to help them gain a lifelong trust in their heavenly Father.

Bengtson's research has led me to comprehend that — even as a grandfather — I must be deliberate in my role with my grandchildren because my influence is greater than I had realized formerly. So what must I be deliberate about? Following are SEVEN key areas I want to share with you! If you think mathematically — like I do, that's one for every day of the week!

ONE: We cannot give our kids what we ourselves do not possess.

I cannot help my offspring become spiritually solid if I am lacking in a solid Biblical foundation myself. A. W. Tozer said:

> *"To admit that there is One who lies beyond us, who exists outside our categories, who will not be dismissed before the*

bar of our reason, nor submit to our curious inquiries; this requires a great deal of humility, more than most of us possess, so we save face, by thinking God down to our level, or at least down to where we can manage Him." He went on to say, *"Many live in the land of Bibles, belonging to churches and laboring to promote the Christian faith. Many live out our entire lives without having given much serious thought about the being of God — gazing in wonder at the I AM. Such thoughts are too difficult, so we choose instead to focus on the betterment of life. Are we secularizing our faith and decaying our inner lives?"* [9]

Does my life reflect a man who has given serious thought about the being of God? Do my children know that — first and foremost — I love God with all my heart and soul and mind and strength? As a dad, we must model lives that reflect this great aim, with daily agendas that include margin to study God's Word and with hearts that are committed to prayer, offering guidance as servant-hearted leaders of our families. Our kids will know us by our priorities — better perhaps than we know ourselves.

TWO: Jump into discipleship (with both feet).

At Veritas Academy, we encourage dads to support their children with the home assignments from our discipleship classes. We want dads to teach, discuss Scripture memory and do the assigned readings together with their kids — especially in the middle and upper grades. I previously taught a discipleship course to junior boys in which we read *Mere Christianity* [25] by C. S. Lewis. This led to great discussions about their walk with Jesus, about marriage, how to treat girls, how to lead well and much more. However, boys, who were able to discuss these topics with their dads, were impacted far greater and contributed more deeply to our discussions in class. I urge you to intentionally set aside time to have personal discussions about life-changing topics with each of your children.

Take the initiative to plan some important spiritual milestone ceremonies for your kids. While getting a driver's license or turning 21 are certainly milestones, also establish milestones with significant lifelong, life-changing and family-oriented meaning. Have discussions about what your family stands for, what it means to be a member of your family historically and what it means for your family today. Ellen's father, a small-town attorney, was honest to a fault. That may seem like a contradiction, but he would overpay his taxes just in case he made a mistake. He would undercharge his clients so that no one could consider him to be unscrupulous. We share stories about him with our kids and grandkids because we want them to see honesty as a virtue our family regards highly.

During the early adolescent years, be intentional about addressing the topic of purity so that your children come to embrace God's plan for love, marriage and sex — in that order. Be deliberately involved with the process of preparing your kids to walk in the standards of purity that God has established. Be the primary source of information and guidance for your kids about the delicate topic of sex. Get past your discomfort, and purpose to make these conversations natural and comfortable. Past mistakes you may have made do not disqualify you. Whether the Lord leads you to share these or not, make sure to become your children's primary source of guidance as they form standards for themselves.

The Jewish culture historically has done a great job of ushering boys and girls into manhood and womanhood. At the age of 12 or 13, a Jewish child was considered an adult and responsible for his or her actions. Even primitive African tribes hold coming-of-age ceremonies, in particular, for their boys. Yet our society defines adolescence as the time between 10 and 19 years of age, and some even extend it to the age of 24. Do what you can do to avoid the pitfall of having the adolescent stage last far too long. Our boys and girls need to mature into adulthood at a reasonable age, and they will need help to counter the low and confusing bar that the media often sets for them. Make sure to identify the character qualities each of your children needs to reach mature adulthood, and then be intentional in your role as their disciple-maker. Most importantly, lead them to personally embrace Jesus as their Lord and Savior because only He can redeem and transform their lives.

THREE: Make a habit of blessing your children.

Another Jewish custom is the blessing of children, with Jewish fathers traditionally blessing each of their boys and girls every Sabbath. When we pray for our children, we are communicating to God on their behalf. A blessing, however, is pronouncing God's favor upon them. Blessing your children is a spoken message of high value extended towards a child, offering up hope for their future. It is a great way to affirm each of your children in specific ways that nurture their unique strengths and point to their God-given identities. We bless our children when we speak strong, encouraging words over them. Our words matter — something I need to remind myself continually. Words tend to just pop out of my mouth; and when they come without deliberate thought, they often are sarcastic or critical. Ephesians 4:29 tells us only to speak words that build up another and give grace. As fathers, we hold a powerful influence over our children. What we say about them either can fuel or diminish vision and life.

I try to bless my grandkids whenever they spend the night at our home, which has become important and meaningful to them and to me. It connects us in powerful ways. At bedtime, I rub their backs and sing calming songs about Jesus to them as well. While I have a terrible singing voice, I must be good at giving back rubs because they willingly listen to me sing. One Sunday, my youngest daughter and her family heard "*There's Something About That Name*" at church. My daughter leaned over to her daughter, Hadassah, and whispered, *"This reminds me of Opa's back rubs!"* After singing, I place my hand on their heads and speak the Levitical blessing over them. Greta, another granddaughter, has it memorized and will remind me if I attempt to slip out without affirming her in this way.

I add a prayer for courage to this ancient blessing found in Numbers 6:24-26. I know that courage comes by way of learning to face tough things. I know that many of the lessons my grandkids will learn will come by way of difficulty and struggle and, therefore, require courage. Before Joshua was to cross the Jordan River and take possession of the land, God commanded him: "*Be strong and courageous. Do not be frightened, and do not be dismayed, for the LORD your God is with you wherever you go*" (Joshua 1:9). Imagine how much courage it took for Joshua to lead his people through water to an unknown land that he was to conquer.

Another way to bless your children is to write them a letter. Not a text. Not an email. A handwritten letter. Just this year, after graduation, a dad came up to me and asked, "Do you remember when you would encourage us to write our children start-of-the-school-year letters?" This father shared that he had written letters to both of his boys at the start of each school year and was amazed to find his graduate had saved every letter. This letter is not an opportunity to share disappointments — "*Last year didn't end very well, but this year hopefully will be different.*" Nor should this letter be a lecture in any form or fashion. Instead it should be about how much you love and value them and how excited you are for this new school year, which will be an opportunity to grow together. Of course, you can suggest setting some goals in gentle ways. Think about the kind of letter you would like to receive from God!

FOUR: Dump the lecture.

When I was young, my dad would sit me down to straighten me out and get me on the right path. Each time, I knew this was going to take a while. Out of respect, I would sit there — like Charlie Brown — with "blah-blah-blahs" spinning around in my head. My dad would realize I wasn't listening; so he would get upset, grab my arm and give me a shake. Often things would escalate from there. I don't remember what he said, but I do remember the angry outbursts between us.

Lectures didn't work back then, and lectures won't work in this generation. In fact, lectures don't work well with anyone at any time. Lecturing merely gives us the illusion that we are doing our part; but if we are to be honest with ourselves, lecturing is easy. It takes no thought to merely spew out our disappointments, frustrations and words of wisdom with a lecture. It may make us feel better, but the benefits stop there.

Instead of lecturing, consider teaching through stories. Use examples from your life. Teach from stories about people you have read about. Use the parables of Jesus. Using real-life examples to teach is a powerful way to maintain influence with your child without making them grow defensive.

When a student needs to chat with me about their behavior or performance, my goal is to talk 10% and have them talk the remaining 90% of the time. I try to come up with some good questions that will guide them towards right thinking and right conclusions themselves. When they give me excuses and rationalizations for their actions, I try to ask more questions that will move them to rethink their actions and come up with solutions themselves for how to make things right. When I am tempted to lecture, I remind myself to *"be quick to hear, slow to speak, slow to anger"* (James 1:19).

Several years ago, a dad came to me and asked, *"Is being dad to a freshman boy supposed to be this painful?"* The first thing I asked him was if he lectured his son a lot. *"Of course. I am the dad, and isn't it my job to pass on all my wisdom?"* We discussed asking the right questions to lead his son towards giving himself the lectures. Later that day, this dad came home from work to find his son muttering *"Oh God"* each time something went wrong on the video game he was playing. Tempted to jump in with a lecture on taking the Lord's Name in vain, he caught himself and went to change clothes while he cooled off. Instead of lecturing his son, he resorted to prayer and asked God for patience and wisdom in guiding his son. Later in the week, while riding in the car together, this dad asked his son, *"Do you know the Ten Commandments?"* The boy explained that, while he did not have them memorized, he knew most of them. The dad then asked him specifically about taking the Lord's Name in vain. As his dad drove along, he couldn't believe what his son said next. *"Yeah Dad, it says we shouldn't use God's Name in vain; and I think I am in the habit of doing that."* After staying silent for a moment, the dad then asked his son to explain further. His son went on to share how he was in a habit of using God's Name in irreverent ways around his friends and even when playing video games. Then the kicker. His son said, *"Dad, I don't want you to point it out in front of my friends; but I have to break this habit. Every time I use God's Name in vain, would you just clear your throat really loud? That can be our signal and hopefully help me break this habit."* This dad concluded our conversation by sharing that it had been the most effective form of a lecture because it was one that his son gave to himself. He had come up with his solution for how to correct this bad habit. The best part is that this dad and son found themselves on the same team with the same aims in mind.

FIVE: Promote virtuous character.

Ellen and I often consider virtues we want our grandkids to gain — like the ones we espoused with our children. Thanks to great thinkers and authors like C. S. Lewis, it's not hard to craft a list. How to guide kids in gaining these virtues is the challenging part. Some character qualities are learned merely by watching, and parents are their primary models. Do we gossip and talk about others poorly? Do we take responsibility for our actions? Do we apologize earnestly when we are wrong? Do we pray and read God's Word regularly? Do we respect others and lead with a servant-hearted mindset? Our children will be the best judges of our virtuous — or lack thereof — character.

Other qualities are gained through practice and still others come by way of encouraging words and wise support. Then there's the growth in virtues that come by way of natural consequences, which cause a child to take responsibility for their actions. Finally, some virtues are formed by way

64

of discomfort and challenge — by being stretched, which never feels good at the time. Learning to be comfortable with this stretching — a discomfort that comes with growth — is an essential character quality to grow virtuous character, especially the more rugged virtues.

Commonly but not exclusively, moms tend towards teaching "softer" virtues like gratitude, kindness, honesty, forgiveness and compassion. Dads often are more likely to teach the more "rugged" virtues like courage, resilience, diligence, temperance and self-denial. We can argue over which list these virtues fall into; but the point I wish to make is that our kids need all of them, and it's important to comprehend how they are being learned and by whom.

Diligence and resilience are two essential virtues to focus on because following the path of least resistance is an all-too-easy habit to fall into. Playing a video game is easier than cleaning one's room. Checking up on social media sites is easier than picking up one's Bible. Cheating is easier than being prepared for a test. Plagiary certainly is a quicker method than coming up with one's own words. C. S. Lewis said:

> *"Every time you make a choice you are turning into the central part of you, the part of you that chooses, into something a little different than it was before. And taking your life as a whole, with all your innumerable choices, all your life long you are slowly turning this central thing into a heavenly creature or a hellish creature...."*[26]

We naturally lean toward what is easiest, what seems most enjoyable right now — that which is least painful and challenging. Searching for a painless, easy path is the wrong aim, however, and a path we will never find. Not every choice our children makes needs to be a difficult one, but the path of least resistance must never become their standard for making decisions. So much is learned in the struggle of learning; so much is missed out on when we choose what is easy instead. Laziness comes easily. Diligence comes with determined practice.

The same can be said for self-centeredness. It comes naturally while self-denial is hard. It's easier to lie than to admit the truth when it serves ME to do so. It's easier to get what I want than to think of others. To remain angry rather than to forgive. To withdraw rather than connect. Aristotle said, *"I count him braver who overcomes his desires than him who conquers his enemies; for the hardest victory is over self."* He considered courage to be the first of human qualities because it guarantees the others.

It's why I often speak of courage as a vital virtue. Courage is about doing what you don't want to do the best you possibly can. Courage is caught. Not taught. As a lifelong basketball coach, there were numerous occasions when I would find my team tied, with only seconds left on the clock. At those times, I looked for the player who most wanted the ball in his or her hands because I knew it would take courage to be the one called on in those tense moments. The courage to take a chance. The courage to face possible disappointment, to potentially be the hero or the goat. The courage to handle the moment with confidence. The courage to not back away. Former President Ronald Reagan claimed, *"There are no easy answers, but there are simple answers. We must have the courage to do what we know is morally right."*

SIX: Love your wife well.

Years ago, I heard James Dobson, founder of Focus on the Family, state that the best thing a father could do for his kids was to show them how much he loves their mother. This really got me questioning myself. I loved my wife and even did nice things for her; but did my kids see me loving their mother well, or did they see me prioritizing them over her? When I came home from work, I would pet the dog, tickle the kids, look at the mail and go change my clothes. Later, when I remembered, I would find my wife and give her a kiss. I doubt my kids saw Ellen as the most important person to me in that instant.

In Ephesians 5, the Apostle Paul challenges husbands to love their wives just as Christ also loved the Church and gave Himself for her. In verse 32, he defines marriage as a profound mystery. Historian and writer, Geoffrey Bromiley wrote, *"As God made man in His own image, so He made earthly marriage in the image of His own eternal marriage with His people."*[27] How profound and difficult to comprehend! There's something about a strong, healthy marriage that provides deep security for our children and perhaps even makes it easier for them to place their security in Christ.

Colossians 3:14 tells us to "put on love" because it is the bond of perfection. Men, God has placed a tall order on us! All the ideas in this chapter are held up by how well we love. I love my wife well when I am seeking God with all my heart. I love my wife well when I take seriously my discipling role with our children. I love my wife well when I listen to her and seek to understand her rather than critique or lecture her. I love my wife well when I open honestly to her — and it takes courage for me to be vulnerable and admit my shortcomings. It certainly takes self-denial because, if you are like me, you would prefer to have your needs met instead of seeking to meet the needs of your wife and children.

It took years for my wife to authentically trust me because she did not really feel loved by me. While I was good at providing financial security and taking care of our home and cars, I did not understand her need for heart security. She worried that someday I would reject her at a time when she could no longer meet my needs. Instead of trying to understand the underlying cause of her worries, I just let her know how dumb it was of her to think this way. Finally, however, the truth hit me over the head. She had come to believe that her value to me rested on what she could do for me — how she performed (a label she had placed on herself as a child). Looking back, I see how I contributed to her worries because I was very good at letting her know when she failed me. Plus, I considered my responsibilities to be more demanding than hers. How could taking care of children be so taxing? Let's just say that I did not affirm her well or show her appreciation; and as a result, she began to grow distant from me. It was safer for her to keep up walls than to draw close to me. It wasn't until I began to love her better that she was willing to truly trust me.

My mom was genuinely servant-hearted. She spent her married years serving my dad, my brother and me. Too much so. This certainly shaped how I viewed the role of a wife and mom. Then at the age of 68, she died of lung cancer — even though she had never smoked in her life. It was difficult to watch her suffer and decline. More difficult, however, was watching how my dad treated her as she grew unable to take care of his needs. I was shocked at how he quit showing her any love or value and instead would leave her to care for her needs as he went out to play golf. He quit loving my mom once she no longer could serve him. God used his reaction to really grab a hold of my heart as I began to realize the correlation to Ellen's worries. Then I watched my dad decline and die a few years later. As my dad was dying, I know he felt much sorrow and shame over how he had treated my mom in the final season of her life. In her last days, he bought her two dozen red roses. These same roses, now wilted and brown, were still in the vase on his table after his death.

To love well is difficult. To define love is not. God's Word tells us what love looks like. Love is patient and kind. Love does not envy or become proud. Love is not rude nor does love seek its own. Love is not easily provoked. Love rejoices in the truth. Love bears all things, believes all things, hopes all things and endorses all things. This is a tall order and one in which we will fail over and over. But by God's grace, we will get better at it, and our families will be blessed as a result.

SEVEN: Pray together.

If you asked Ellen how I best show love to her, her answer would have to do with prayer. She feels loved and secure when she knows I pray for her. The opposite is also true. If I want her to trust me, she needs to know that the guidance and direction I provide is rooted in prayer. As her husband and as the father of our children, I am called to be a man of prayer. A sign in our garage reminds me to take time to do certain things — like laugh, which is the music of the soul. The very last line is "take time to pray, for it is the greatest power on earth." I need constant reminders to turn my eyes upward and to *"continue steadfastly in prayer, being watchful in it..."* (Colossians 4:2), which is not only the greatest power but also my most important role.

Not only am I to pray for my wife and children, I also need to pray with them. When I start out the day praying with Ellen, I then know what is on her heart and how to pray for her throughout the day. Praying together links our hearts and our days. I used to neglect doing this because I made it too complicated. Now I just wrap my arms around Ellen before leaving in the morning; then she prays first, and I follow afterwards. We start out the day together in this way, which gives me a glimpse into what is on my wife's heart that day. I pay attention to her prayers and purpose to ask her about these requests later in the day. You can do the same with your children. Praying together provides a great way to communicate together with God.

The devil will do anything to distract us from praying — perhaps because he is in the business of breaking up families, and he knows that prayer holds families together. It's true. Getting distracted from prayer is the enemy's chief aim with us because prayer is a powerful force, uniting us with God and with each other. Praying couples are far more apt to stay together. Many studies have been done on divorce in Christian homes, which is occurring at higher and higher percentages than previous generations. But the divorce rate for couples who pray together is incredibly lower than for those who don't pray together. The statistics I have read are astoundingly clear. Praying together makes a vast difference.

Our Practices

CHAPTER FOUR

The Power in Our Words

"Words are the most powerful thing in the universe...
Words are containers.
They contain faith or fear, and they produce after their
kind."[28]

— Charles Capps, an English Bible teacher

Our school headmaster, Jef Fowler, reminds our students that they are to *"focus on — and cultivate mastery over — the only three things in this world that they alone completely control: their attitude, their effort and their tongue."* He explains that their attitude determines the joy and satisfaction they find in life and, at the same time, can limit their possibilities. Their effort determines where they will reside within that realm of possibilities; yet their tongue has the power to destroy, in an instant, what they have spent countless hours building.

Because our words can either build or destroy that which we set out to accomplish, I have devoted an entire chapter to this topic. The words we speak, the words we hear and even the words that tumble around in our minds strongly influence attitudes — both positively and negatively. Our words matter. They change us, and they change others. Our words can produce joy in others, or they can produce fear. They can build connection or establish distance.

Words can carry influence that moves forward with a life of their own, whirling in the minds of hearers — sometimes even affecting perspectives for years on end. Some of my father's words — spoken in moments of anger — suddenly pop up when I begin to feel insecure and doubt my abilities. "*You're good for nothing*" begins to flow out of my subconscious mind, hampering hope and igniting anxiety. Words spoken over me as a child propelled me into years of striving to be valued by others. They created a false view of my experiences. As I learned to ponder the words of Jesus instead and allowed them to replace the negative thoughts, my anxious striving began to dissolve. Words never truly die, but they fade and lose their impact as the words of Jesus grow louder. We all know the old saying, "*Sticks and stones can break your bones, but words can never harm you.*" More real is: "*The tongue has no bones but is strong enough to break a heart.*"

Attitude. Effort. Tongue. These three things in life we can cultivate mastery over. How well we, as parents, master our tongues has a strong influence over how well our children learn to master their attitude, their effort and words they speak. Our words can influence whether a child will listen to our guidance and correction or reject what we have to say. The words we speak can have a lasting impact, creating either good or bad memories. Words, which may not mean much to you, can remain in the heart and mind of someone else for years.

Death or Life (Proverbs 18:21)

God created the world with His Word. "*In the beginning was the Word, and the Word was with God, and the Word was God*" (John 1:1). We create vision and hope for our children with affirming words. To affirm someone is to declare something to be true, which can breathe encouragement into a child in need of it. Just like us, our children need hope, especially when they struggle or fail or make a bad choice. When my 14-year-old granddaughter Kate was younger, her parents would look her in the eye and say, "*You are smart. You are capable. You are strong*" each time she would act insecure about her abilities or shrink back from a task. Not only would they say these words to her, but they would make her repeat them as well. Today she is a confident, strong student and competitor. These words have come to define her.

When a grandchild of mine is struggling, I try to think of Biblical truths to speak over them. You are a child of God. You are fearfully and wonderfully made. God has a plan for you. Your sins are paid by Jesus. Cast your burdens on Jesus because He cares for you. God's Word has the power to create renewed hope and life because it is "...*living and active, sharper than any two-edged sword...*" (Hebrews 4:12).

> "*A word fitly spoken is like apples of gold in a setting of silver*"
> (Proverbs 25:11).

Words can also destroy. Joyce Meyer wisely said, "*Words are containers for power; you choose what kind of power they carry.*"[29] James understood it as well when he crafted his letter to Jewish Christians who were living in social and spiritual conflict outside of Palestine. Anger and despair abounded; so James reminded them to be "...*quick to hear, slow to speak, slow to anger*" (James 1:19). Later in his letter, he wrote, "... *how great a forest is set ablaze by such a small fire! And the tongue is a fire, a world of unrighteousness. The tongue is set among our members, staining the whole body, setting on fire the entire course of life, and set on fire by hell*" (James 3:5-6).

I find it easy to control my tongue when my days are clicking along smoothly, but the real test comes when I face disappointment or hurt. An anonymous person wisely said, "*Don't mix bad words with your bad mood. You'll have many opportunities to change a mood, but you'll never get the opportunity to replace the words you spoke.*" When I am tempted to speak out of anger or hurt or disappointment, I know that a wiser plan is to pause and pray instead. Especially during tumultuous times and during conflict, it's good to remember: "*A gentle tongue is a tree of life, but perverseness in it breaks the spirit*" (Proverbs 15:4).

Anxiety or Strength

Words can nurture anxiety and fear, OR they can foster strength and hopefulness. Consider the kind of language that your children regularly hear in your home. Do they hear a language of judgment or a language of affirmation? A language of anxiety or a language of peace? A language of fear or one of courage? A language of discouragement or a language of hope? We currently live in a very anxious culture — one that feels quite out of control. We have real reasons to feel anxious; yet we have every reason to hope. Our God is sovereign and unchanging. He is over all that is taking place. How we choose to respond to our fears will greatly influence how our children respond to theirs. Could we be fueling anxious attitudes by speaking too often about stress? Are challenging experiences often described as *overwhelming* or *stressful* or considered to be *too much?* Does speaking about challenges in this way cause our children to grow more anxious instead of learning how to wisely face them?

I remember times as a college student when I would stay up all night to type a term paper due the next day. Unlike computers, typing on a manual typewriter required precision, and precision was a skill I lacked. The experience would have been vastly easier had I been able to delete or autocorrect my mistakes. Instead I would painstakingly brush over a mistake with white-out, wait for it to dry and then type the correct spelling over the white blotch. Too many mistakes led to throwing out an entire page — something which frequently happened. Such frustrations were normal challenges to work through rather than grow anxious about, and my skills and confidence grew as I learned to navigate them well. Our entire lives are filled with both smooth and challenging experiences. How our children learn to respond to challenges is influenced by how these experiences are viewed and spoken about.

Correction or Criticism

Learning how to receive and apply correction is important. The Bible tells us: "*Hear instruction and be wise, and do not neglect it*" (Proverbs 8:33).

Furthermore, when we listen to reproof, we gain intelligence. (Proverbs 15:32) We are to diligently train our children; but unless our words fall on hearts that are both teachable and reachable, our influence will have little effect. The flavor of our words is key. *"Let your speech always be gracious, seasoned with salt ... "* (Colossians 4:6) is wise advice not only with others but with our children as well. We are to be salt and light, extending kindness by our words that display both God's truth and His grace. Kindness has a way of softening even the hardest of hearts so that what we have to say is both heard and received.

How do we disciple our children in ways that they are more likely to hear and not neglect our teaching? I believe that another key also has to do with how we state our opinions. We can criticize or we can correct, both resulting in decidedly different outcomes. Criticism points to what a child has done wrong, looking back to what already has taken place. *"I just cleaned our car, and your dirty shoes messed it up again."* Like children, my defenses want to flare up when criticized — as do my justifications. Correction, on the other hand, is about what you want someone to do moving forward. *"When your shoes are muddy, please remember to take them off before climbing into the car"* would likely elicit a better response. It is the same expectation but in a gentler, more receptive way. Here are a few examples of how to turn your criticisms into corrections.

Criticism: *You failed this test because you didn't study enough.*

Correction: *How will you study better for the next test so that you get better results?*

Criticism: *You missed this problem because you copied down the numbers wrong.*

Correction: *You will get the right answer when you copy the numbers down correctly.*

Criticism: *Your essay is messy and poorly written. I can't help you edit it.*

Correction: *I will help you edit your essay once it's legible and you have put more thought into writing it.*

Criticism: *Stop running in the kitchen.*

Correction: *Remember to walk when you go through the kitchen.*

Criticism: *Stop arguing and complaining.*

Correction: *I will listen to you when you speak respectfully.*

One word of wisdom I consider priceless has to do with timing – to keep the first five to 10 minutes of each day free of any criticism or correction. When the day starts positive, it has a far better chance of staying that way. As your children's teacher, disciple-maker, mentor and coach, you undoubtedly have many lessons you wish for them to learn. You have been granted the wonderful opportunity to parent them wisely as you care for their well-being. Your season of time with them will end sooner than you think, so don't waste your words. *"Let no corrupting talk come out of your mouths, but only such as is good for building up, as fits the occasion, that it may give grace to those who hear"* (Ephesians 4:29).

Shame or Heal

What do we gain in pointing out what is wrong with others? Part of our human nature seems to enjoy "gotcha" moments all too much! Perhaps at times we do this to make ourselves feel better. When it comes to our children, they certainly need their mistakes pointed out and a firm hand of discipline from time to time; but how we approach these times determines both their receptiveness and our influence. One all-too-common approach is to expose sin and then shame a child into repentance. We point out their mistakes and then make our children feel badly about what they have done. Shame is a disconnector, however. Shame promotes fear and withdrawal to avoid more pain. If you are prone to saying, *"Shame on you,"* this might be your style. Shame is different from guilt, however. Guilt is present when I recognize my wrongdoing and have a need to be forgiven. Shame makes me want to hide because I am sad over who I am. Guilt moves me to the cross of Christ, while shame tends to move the cross further away.

Jesus never used shame to get people to follow Him or to correct someone. Instead He revealed sin and immediately moved towards restoration. One example can be found in John 8:7 when the Pharisees wanted to expose and shame a woman caught in adultery. Jesus addressed their plan to stone her by saying, "*Let him who is without sin among you be the first to throw a stone at her.*" After they all left, Jesus told the woman, "*Neither do I condemn you; go, and from now on sin no more*" (John 8:11). He acknowledged her sin and exhorted her to stop, but He did not condemn her.

How do we carry out the "reveal and heal" approach to discipline with our children? First, we make ourselves safe for them to share openly and be honest with us. We do this by listening and seeking to understand what they are thinking and feeling. Seeking to understand does not imply we agree, however. Then we validate their feelings by accurately stating back what they are feeling — something we glean by listening well. Naming their emotions makes children feel known and more willing to admit mistakes. Next we offer solutions and guidance as well as encouragement to recover from what they have done. We facilitate repentance by keeping the weight of responsibility on our children for their poor choices but mentoring, supporting and affirming them in the process. The goal is to maintain an unshakable relationship with them that remains steady and loving — regardless of their behavior.

Unify or Divide

What we say about — or to — each other either fosters unity or distance. This is true for both kids and adults. To encourage unity among believers in the Ephesian Church, Paul wrote, "*Let no corrupting talk come out of your mouths, but only such as is good for building up, as fits the occasion, that it may give grace to those who hear. And do not grieve the Holy Spirit of*

God, by whom you were sealed for the day of redemption. Let all bitterness and wrath and anger and clamor and slander be put away from you, along with all malice. Be kind to one another, tenderhearted, forgiving one another, as God in Christ forgave you" (Ephesians 4:29-32).

The Bible tells us to speak in ways that build up and encourage unity. We are to let go of slander and clamor and malice, which can harm the reputation of others and destroy relationships. No wonder Jesus said that *"people will give account for every careless word they speak"* (Matthew 12:36). What our children hear us say about their teachers influences their willingness to listen and learn in the classroom. How they hear us speak about other children influences how they relate to them. Likewise, what teachers say among themselves about students and their parents impacts opinions and alters behavior. Our words can cause great harm or great good because our words impact beliefs about others. They form narratives — true, false, good or bad — by which others are viewed. Here are some questions to ask and teach your children to ask as well before talking about others:

- Is what I am about to share true?

- Is it necessary to share?

- Why do I want to share it?

- What do I want the person I am sharing it with to do about the information?

- Would sharing this information foster unity, reconciliation or division?

What if we were to make *honor* the flavor of our language regarding every family member? What if we were to establish *honor* as the way we communicate about each other in our school community as well? Honor means being both truthful and affirming as we talk through conflict. Honor requires humility — that we admit our mistakes and forgive others for theirs. Honor means treating each person with respect and value — even when we disagree. Honor, therefore, fosters unity and connectedness. Our words truly have the power to unify or cause division.

Grateful or Grumbling

Choosing to be grateful daily will change your attitude like nothing else. So will a grumbling mindset. We simply cannot grumble and be grateful at the same time because one chases out the other. We, therefore, must make a deliberate choice between a grumbling mindset or a grateful one. Years ago, very early in my role as a school administrator, I found myself growing very anxious and discouraged. The more I focused on my troubles, the more I grumbled about them. God's Word started to speak to me in this area, however, as I read Scriptures like we: *"enter his gates with thanksgiving, and his courts with praise..."* (Psalm 100:4) and *"give thanks in all circumstances..."* (1 Thessalonians 5:18). So I decided to give it a try. I began to intentionally start each day with praise and thanksgiving to God. This simple change has made all the difference to the quality of my days. Regardless of what I see on my daily agenda, I choose to thank God for the opportunity it provides. Regardless of what happened the day before, I choose to put it aside and set my mind on things above. Beginning each day with an attitude of gratitude before the Lord has transformed my life into peace-filled days.

> *"Keep ascending the mountain of cheerfulness by daily scattering seeds of kindness along the way as best you can, and should mists hide the mountaintop, continue undaunted and you will reach the sun-tipped heights in your own life-experience."*
>
> — Unknown

Laughter and Joy

Like gratitude, laughter and joy are restorative. Smiling and laughter have been found to strengthen the immune system and even reduce blood pressure. At times, all we and our children need is a good laugh, which can relax and open the door to joy. Worries can't hang around a joyful mood. King Solomon, known as the wisest king, is the one who said, *"A joyful heart is good medicine, but a crushed spirit dries up the bones"* (Proverbs

17:22). Shared laughter is known to relieve tension and build bonds – an open door to deeper connection. Studies indicate that humor (but not sarcasm) reduces stress — similarly to physical exercise. After a tense situation is resolved with your child, rather than dwell on it, reframe what occurred lightheartedly to rebuild a positive attitude. Benjamin Franklin was known for many wise sayings, including, "*Trouble knocked at the door, but, hearing laughter, hurried away.*"

Unspoken Words

My friend Sarah nearly resigned from her job because she felt like she was doing a poor job and was going to be fired. Her employer was shocked and disappointed that she wanted to quit, but he had failed to express his appreciation for her or give her credit for a job well done. At the same time, Sarah was struggling to connect with her teenage daughter who had stopped confiding in her. Later through counseling, Sarah discovered that her daughter felt mostly disapproval from her mother; so she began to distance herself out of self-protection. Like Sarah, her daughter was desperate for words of affirmation, words they seldom heard. As Sarah changed the flavor of her words, the distance between them began to evaporate.

At the same time, Sarah gained an understanding for why her boss did not affirm her. Like her, he did not have the mental space to think about affirming others because he was so focused on his tasks. Likewise, he did not recognize the importance of expressing appreciation — just as Sarah had not recognized the importance of painting hope and vision for her daughter. Instead both were focused on fixing problems and getting things done. The absence of affirmation led to false narratives out of which they acted.

We all need words of affirmation. When we feel valued, good things follow. Individuals who feel valued and respected are less likely to complain or grumble. Conversely, they are more likely to comply and face challenges with confident attitudes. Words of encouragement, especially during struggling times, help them gain the willingness to rise and try again. They learn to see opportunities in their difficulties rather than the other way around. Words left unspoken can leave behind holes of doubt and worry.

Is my teacher disappointed in me?

Does my father find me unlovable?

Does my mom think I can't be successful?

Does my boss think I am failing?

Feelings of despair come when one's heart is empty of encouragement. Then a bankrupt heart leads to a loss of enthusiasm. Your son or daughter can lose everything but enthusiasm and still be able to rise to success. Their enthusiasm and zest for life rise and fall with how encouraged and valued they feel.

We speak with unspoken words with our body as well. We speak acceptance or rejection. Warmth or coldness. Delight or frustration. Often what our children hear with their ears is what they *see* us saying. Do we show value to them by giving them eye contact? Does our face display warmth or coldness? Delight or disdain? We all smile in the same language.

Thoughts

To change how you feel about a situation, begin by changing how you think about it. Neuroscientists call this technique *cognitive reappraisal,* which can make stressful circumstances feel less threatening. I grow an anxious attitude when I allow my mind to whirl with fear-driven or angry thoughts. The more I allow this kind of self-talk to brew, the more it begins to influence my choices and actions. Our enemy knows that our lives will move in the direction of our loudest thoughts; so his most effective weapon formed against us is to deceive us in our minds, where our battles against spiritual forces of evil take place. (Ephesians 6:12) The evil one understands that he can break a person down with negative thoughts. Even a few words whirling around in my mind can make me feel defeated.

Thinking is a skill — and not just something that happens to us, however. We all need to gain the self-awareness that our thinking process interprets and personalizes what happens but does not necessarily reflect reality. We tend to interpret what we hear and what we think through our experiences and then personalize these thoughts through our needs and unresolved hurts. Just because we think something does not mean it's true. Thankfully, we have the gift of the Holy Spirit, who will guide us into intentional ways to think about our thinking. That is Biblical metacognition. We "...take *every thought captive to obey Christ*" (2 Corinthians 10:5). We choose to think about what is true, honorable, just, pure, lovely and commendable. (Philippians 4:8) In doing so, we are being transformed by the renewing of our minds. (Romans 12:2)

What we choose to think about determines the attitude of our minds. That's why our children need to develop filters that prevent harmful thoughts from taking root so that they develop strong minds, gaining victory over the schemes of the devil. The best filter is a healthy Biblical understanding of who God is and who He created us to become. Their minds will be renewed by thinking rightly about God, themselves and others. The same is true for us! The clearer I think, the clearer I will see and am able to "*destroy arguments and every lofty opinion raised against the knowledge of God...*" (2 Corinthians 10:5).

I must be deliberate to not get distracted in my thoughts when I settle in to pray and meditate on God's Word in the morning. I need my phone out of sight so that I won't be informed of the incoming text, call or notification; and I need to stay out of my email inbox. Instead I must deliberately choose to turn my first thoughts to prayer and meditation on His Word. I know that renewal in my mind takes place as His voice begins to take up more space in my thinking than other thoughts, which quickly want to fill up the space instead.

When one of my grandkids makes a poor choice, I ask them whose voice they are listening to and thinking about. William must have been giving this some thought. One day this summer, he rushed into my kitchen saying, "*Oma, you have to read Romans 7! There is a battle going on in my mind. It's like the devil is sitting on one of my shoulders, telling me to do bad things; but Jesus is on the other shoulder, telling me to follow Him instead. All I have to do is turn and listen to Jesus, and I will do the right thing!*" I am watching him grow more and more consistent in making better decisions as a result. As a young boy who wants to be good but struggles with impulsive actions, these verses give him confidence and assurance that he does not walk alone but has a Helper who is always with him.

To summarize this chapter, here's a favorite saying from *Apples of Gold*, a 1962 compilation of quotes by Jo Petty:

> *You can't control the length of your life — but you can control its width and depth.*
>
> *You can't control the contour of your face — but you can control its expression.*
>
> *You can't control the weather — but you can control the atmosphere of your mind.*
>
> *Why worry about things you can't control when you can keep yourself busy controlling the things that depend on you?*[30]

CHAPTER FIVE

Parenting &
Teaching Your
Challenging Child

"Don't doubt your value. Don't run from who you are."[31]
C. S. Lewis, *The Chronicles of Narnia*

Children are uniquely created. Each one. Each child has been intricately formed by God with a unique blend of both strengths and weaknesses. Each child requires an individually tailored parenting approach to address the unique challenges he or she presents. In partnership schools like the University-Model®, parents can work individually with their children at home. At the same time, they can partner with school educators, who inform parents of how their children interact with their peers and other like-minded adults in a school setting. A parent of five children had this to say:

> *Being a part of Veritas Academy has given me the gift of knowing my children. My five children span 10 grades. They are completely different people — each with unique struggles and strengths. I was initially drawn to this model because I knew that I needed structure, but we also craved time and flexibility. Veritas gave me a place to hold my children to a high standard while being intimately involved in their educational process.*

*On the best days, my proximity has paved the way for encour-
agement and support (even though there are certainly days that
I make a mess of things!). The proximity has allowed me to
better discern the things the kids need in each season — not
just academically but socially, emotionally and spiritually. My
husband and I are constantly syncing up and readjusting as we
work out how to best shepherd each of our children through
our rhythms, activities, conversations and goals. It's a lens that
guides our prayers and our parenting. Veritas has given me a
space to really know my children and to put that knowing into
action. I believe this reflects the way that God parents us. It's
an honor and a privilege to partner with Him during this relatively short season as we guide, encourage, correct and equip
these young people that God has asked us to parent.*

Parenting and teaching our children can be difficult work and especially so with challenging children. All children challenge us in ways but
some more than others. This chapter is about those challenging children
who weaken our resolve, test our limits and shake our confidence as their
parents. In this chapter, you will find sections full of ideas on parenting:

- The Strong-Willed Child
- The Unmotivated Child
- The Anxious Child
- The Angry Child
- The Perfectionist Child
- The Dishonest Child
- The Argumentative Child

THE STRONG-WILLED CHILD

*"Healthy parenting can be boiled down to those two essential
ingredients: love and control. They must operate in a system of*

checks and balances. Any concentration on love to the exclusion of control usually breeds disrespect and contempt. Conversely, an authoritarian and oppressive home atmosphere is deeply resented by the child who feels unloved or even hated. The objective for the toddler years is to strike a balance between mercy and justice, affection and authority, love and control."
— James Dobson, *The New Strong-Willed Child*[32]

Do you have kids who refuse to comply and test your limits over and over? Do they argue and push to do things their way? Headstrong kids can be very challenging to train; yet they are terrific kids to raise. These determined, persistent kids will be the courageous leaders of tomorrow. We must intentionally guide and shape their character — yet mindfully preserve their passion and energy. Striking a balance between love and control, as Dr. Dobson stated above, is vital during all stages of a child's life and not just in the toddler years — although this balance shifts as the child ages. Walking affectionately in authority is key to maintaining influence and relationship with your children at any age — and especially with those who have an iron will.

I personally believe that God has created many headstrong kids with an iron will for this generation — *"for such a time as this"* (Esther 4:14). These strong-willed kids are destined to become adults who stand for what is right and true. Our role is not to merely tame their spirited natures but to direct their driven personalities in a God-honoring direction. Will, my 10-year-old grandson, stands out as the poster child for strong-willed boys. Little did his parents realize how aptly they named him. His cousin Asa is also strong willed. They can be the best of friends — as well as the fiercest of enemies — when their opinions clash. I can witness their interactions each week when they spend a school day at home with me. I regularly remind them that love *"does not insist on its own way"* (1 Corinthians 13:5), and they are slowly beginning to comprehend what this truth means!

What characteristics classify them as strong-willed? They struggle to comply when asked to do something they don't want to do. When their hearts are set on something else, they have a very hard time switching gears. They test limits over and over and live at full throttle all day long. They want to call the shots and lead in everything. Rather than accept instruction, they would prefer to learn how to do things themselves. They earnestly want to govern themselves (and others!) — even at their young age. They are argumentative. They experience big, passionate emotions. Teaching them can be challenging!

Kids with iron wills may not be easy to parent, but their determination and never-give-up attitude are also delightful. Their enthusiastic mindset adds life and energy to others and to teams they play on. On numerous occasions, I have watched Will turn the tempo up for his entire soccer team when that needs to happen. Strong-willed kids love challenges. They are born to be future leaders; but as young kids, they tend towards being tyrannical and insisting on their way — regardless of how they get it.

How can we effectively parent and teach our strong-willed kids? Here are a few tips and insights to guide you in rearing these treasures with whom God has blessed us!

TIP 1: AVOID power struggles.

Whatever you do, don't step into a power struggle. A power struggle is any argument with which your strong-willed child will try to engage you that you simply can't win. And they know it! They look for ways to engage you in these unwinnable battles that simply leave you worn out and angry from trying like:

Try to make me care.

Try to make me work hard.

Try to make me eat.

Try to make me stop arguing.

Try to make me admit I lied.

Trying to force compliance in areas that you really can't control simply leaves you frustrated in trying. Plus, it undermines your child's ability to make moral choices based on what is right and wrong or even be held accountable for their actions. Force sets you up for a battle of control that you likely will not gain. I have heard it said that "arguing with a strong-willed child is like mud wrestling with a pig. You both get dirty, and the pig loves it!"

TIP 2: Stay calm and controlled.

Instead stay calm and controlled. When you lose control of your emotions, you essentially are handing over control to them. Causing an adult to melt down gives a child the sense of power and victory — something they crave. Do you find yourself yelling at your kids because it seems to work? It may work in the short term, but anger does not produce any authentic change — except to harden the heart. "...*let every person be quick to hear, slow to speak, slow to anger; for the anger of man does not produce the righteousness of God*" (James 1:19-20). Instead pray! Address your kids once emotions have calmed down. Wait until their passions are no longer fueled by frustration. Gaining your rightful say as their parents will require patient, wise deliberation; but pressuring them into immediate compliance only strengthens their resolve to win the next battle.

TIP 3: Know what you can control.

If you think you can control your kids, think again. There's much as parents that we can control, but to control another person is not one of them. You may be able to force them to comply; but their thoughts, attitudes and desires are outside your control. It's wiser to focus on what you can control: your expectations, your responses and choices and the consequences you extend for both good and bad choices. For example, let them know that you help kids with schoolwork who are first trying themselves. You do not argue with the child who is screaming at you, but you may choose to reward a child who is being respectful. You remove video game privileges from the child who has not completed his work.

Ultimatums lose their effectiveness and give strong-willed kids a challenge to work around. It's best to drop the *"if you don't do this, I will…"* — type comments and the *"if you do this, you will get …."* These types of statements feel like control — something a strong-willed child fights against. Ultimately, you want the child to understand the connection between their choices and consequences — something over which they must gain control. *"Kids who clean their rooms can go out to play"* gives the control to the child. The message that *"you are responsible to make good choices"* is an important one for them to learn.

TIP 4: Speak with vision and affirmation.

Speak vision into your kids. Let them know you believe in who they are becoming. *"I see that you are learning how to be a gracious leader."* Remind them that future leaders must learn how to follow others if they are to become effective leaders themselves. Learning to follow others does not come naturally for strong-willed kids, so watch for times when you can affirm them for leading well.

These kids need opportunities to be trusted again; they need to know you still believe in them. Every day is a new day to prove they can be trustworthy. One step at a time, one lesson learned at a time sets them up to become trustworthy adults. They also need opportunities to be in charge when appropriate. Being the youngest in his family, Will loves to teach his younger cousins; so on days when he has the time, I give him a lesson or two to oversee with a younger child. Ironically, Will expects very high standards of both work and behavior — ones over which he has argued with me in past years when they were expected of him!

TIP 5: Set clear, firm expectations ahead of time.

All kids need boundaries and limits that are clearly defined. Strong-willed kids are more likely to push on fuzzy expectations because they want to know the limits. They figure them out by testing. Clear boundaries settle these kids. Knowing what to expect gives them opportunities to consider wise choices and responses. Just like a clear rubric for a school project is necessary for a student to perform well, the same is true for what we expect regarding behavior. At the same time, it's important to establish only the boundaries your child needs and give them freedom to choose when appropriate within these boundaries. For example, the expectation for my grandkids on their school days with me is that they will accurately complete all the home assignments before the school day ends. However, as they age, I give more and more choice as to when they will accomplish which assignments.

Many kids — and especially those with iron wills — struggle to switch gears from what they are doing to what they need to be doing. To help them transition, consider giving them advance warnings and reminders of how you expect them to respond. With young kids, their first response might be oppositional to being told what to do. They impulsively respond with their strong feelings. At those times, I say something like, *"Show me how you would respond if I gave you another chance."*

TIP 6: Respond early. Don't warn.

Strong-willed kids will take you to your limit each time. If you are prone to giving three warnings, it will take three warnings for them to comply. They know exactly how far they can push you. The solution is to respond early and stop warning. Tell them clearly what you want them to do, and expect them to hear and understand. A habit of repeated warning sets up a cycle in which the parent warns repeatedly, then eventually overreacts out of frustration. Then, after overreacting, the parent feels regret and goes back to ignoring and warning. The child has figured out this cycle. The solution is to say what you mean and mean what you say, which builds trust in your word.

In closing, maintain your child's sense of trust and promote their co-operation. Guide them in ways that maintain their God-given, passionate personalities — traits they need to become the strong leaders God has created them to be. They need a balance of mercy and justice, with parents who are in loving control.

THE UNMOTIVATED CHILD

Today is your opportunity to build the tomorrow you want. [33]

— Ken Poirot

Each spring, I lack the desire to deep clean our outdoor kitchen; but I am determined to get it done by Memorial Day — in time for the summer pool season. There's a distinct difference between motivation and determination that kids need to grasp. Your children won't always feel motivated to do something, but they can still learn to be determined to complete tasks — even those they dislike. Sometime during their years of schooling, you may start to notice a lack of motivation and a willingness to work in your child's attitude towards school — or any kind of work for that matter. Maybe your child lacks the enthusiasm to learn new things, or maybe your child's answer to everything is: *"I don't care"* or *"it doesn't matter."* Or perhaps your child simply is not willing to try, and you have no idea how to help him or her even try. Everyone is motivated; however, some are just motivated toward apathy and laziness. Others toward ease and comfort. For some, the motivation is to resist, to do things their way and not yours. Their motivation is to retain power; and this is especially true for the strong-willed child and even the perfectionist child, who would prefer not to try than risk trying and possibly not be "good enough." Withholding effort is a way to feel in charge. If something feels too hard, an *"I don't care"* attitude could be their way of solving struggles they regularly face. Statements like "*I don't care*" take the pressure off them and make them feel in control.

The key is to turn their negative motivation into a positive one. They resist by acting out on the inside. It takes a lot of energy to resist and withhold, however. Emotionally, it is exhausting. How do we turn their negative motivation into a positive one and effectively help our unmotivated child begin to put effort and energy into their tasks? Following are some helpful TIPS.

TIP 1: Consider if there is an underlying issue.

For a few kids, a thorough battery of testing could be in order. Or perhaps your son or daughter has not developed the skills needed to thrive. When your child encounters difficulties, the reaction may be to stop trying with a task that feels overwhelming. Other kids learn a habit of helplessness. They give up because what they are doing is not working. Their behavior is a strategy to deal with the stress they may feel. With kids like this, it is important to identify the missing skill. Perhaps it is learning to use time well or organizational skills. Some kids struggle with starting an assignment while others struggle to finish. With a little success, more success is likely to follow. Once they get a taste of improvement, they may be motivated to do more. Growth promotes growth.

TIP 2: Consider your child's unique learning style.

Are they an auditory or a visual learner? Some children learn best by movement, and others learn through music. Some think through talking things out, while others think through questioning and logic. Discovering how God has uniquely wired your child is an important step in helping them grow motivated to learn. I highly recommend Dr. Kathy Koch's book, *8 Great Smarts*[34], which is an excellent resource that has helped many parents discover how their children learn best.

TIP 3: Take the electronics out of your child's room.

Withdrawing to their rooms to play video games can be very enticing for some kids; and at the same time, it can cause them to become unmotivated towards any other activities. Video games are intentionally made to draw in kids and hold them. For kids who already struggle with the challenges of learning, technology can make it even harder. Therefore, establish wise boundaries about where your child can use technology and for how long it can be used. Except for school-related tasks, keep their school time free of screens, which somehow make any other task seem to be unpleasant.

TIP 4: Privileges should be earned with responsible behavior.

Ten-year-old William is now in fifth grade, which means he and his parents have ongoing access to grades in all subjects. Suddenly he has grown motivated to study for tests; whereas before, he was unmotivated to do so. It's taken a while to get here; but finally, the light bulb has turned on, regarding the connection between responsible behavior and good outcomes. He is learning that putting effort into his studies produces higher marks! The same lesson should hold true for privileges. For example, video games or playing with friends are a privilege in which they can engage once schoolwork is completed. Free time happens once their rooms are picked up and cleaned. The important message is that responsible behavior or choices bring about good consequences, and the reverse is also true. This alone can turn an unmotivated child around.

Link their choices today to the kind of future they want. Talk about the things they want in the future and have conversations about what it would take to attain those things. Finally, be careful not to overindulge by giving them what they want without having to work for them. Learning to be responsible is the key to the freedom they seek.

TIP 5: Refrain from shouting or arguing.

Shouting shows that you have run out of solutions and gives your child's resisting behavior more power and motivation to continue. Say something like: "*I can't make you do this, and it's important to me because I care about what is good for you.*" Let them know you are for them and not against them. You are on their team and want the best for them.

TIP 6: Refrain from over-helping.

Acting helpless is a way to get other people to do things for you. A grandson of mine will try that at times. The other day, he told me that the word *resilient* was not in his dictionary. He tried convincingly to solicit my help in finding it. I knew he had developed the necessary dictionary skills but didn't like to look up words, so I replied with "*nice try.*" I continued to ignore his grumbling until finally he gave up and found the word himself. Kids learn early on that when they give up or act helpless that someone might step in and help. While looking up the word felt a bit difficult, I knew that expecting him to do something a bit stretching was necessary for him to grow.

TIP 7: Set mini-deadlines throughout the day.

I break the school days for my grandkids into sessions, with clear expectations in each and breaks between. This allows me to motivate them as the day moves along. (See TIP #1 in Chapter 7.) I encourage them to see how much they can accomplish well during each session and then reward them with a break or snack. "*When this assignment is done, you may go out to play*" teaches the concept of working hard in order to have time for doing what they would like to do.

THE ANXIOUS CHILD

> "*Anxiety does not empty tomorrow of its sorrows, but only empties today of its strength.*"[35]
>
> — *Charles Spurgeon*

Being anxious and having anxious kids feel normal today. Recent events in our world certainly have contributed to our anxious culture. Anxiety, however, makes one tense; and tension destroys joy. When joy is gone, our faith is eroded as well. Worries are not just upsetting thoughts but also can make a person feel bad. Some kids get tummy aches or headaches. Others grow shaky or dizzy with pounding hearts. At times, therapy is necessary; but this chapter addresses how to effectively lessen normal childhood fears and worries.

What I worry about can be either a real or perceived threat. Previously, I considered my worrying as an indicator that I somehow cared more deeply. Plus, it gave me a false sense of control because I mistakenly saw worrying as something worthy to do. All that my worries and fears did, however, were to make me anxious. The more I worried, the higher my anxiety grew. Our human nature is inclined to worry, which is why Scriptures repeatedly address worry. Growing convicted by His Word, I began to ask myself questions like:

- Are my kids really safer because I worry?

- Do I keep bad things from happening when I worry?

- Do my worries really mean I care more?

Deep down inside, I knew the answers to these questions were all a resounding NO. That's when I realized the prideful folly in my thinking, learned to pray and gave my worries over to Jesus instead.

Anxiety is about a general sense of fear over something — an anticipation that something bad might happen. Of course, sometimes bad things do happen. COVID happened. Car wrecks happen. People lose their jobs. People die. Kids fail tests. The dog eats their homework! (That happened with one of my grandkids!) Our anxiety often results less from thinking about what could go wrong and more from wanting to control it! When you really stop to think about it, most of the things you worry about never happen; and when they do, you figure out how to get through them. I often remind myself to *"not be anxious about tomorrow, for tomorrow will be anxious for itself. Sufficient for the day is its own trouble"* (Matthew 6:34).

Here are some helpful TIPS to help you and your children worry less.

TIP 1: Make a worry list, and establish a plan to address them.

Help your kids define their worries. Doing so will keep anxiety at bay. Kids commonly worry about:

- What others think.

- Disappointing someone or falling short of expectations.

- Getting hurt or sick themselves or someone they care about.

- Not feeling they can do something well enough.

- Being made fun of or getting embarrassed.

- Rejection.

After making a list, help them address their fears one by one — over time. The Rev. Dr. Martin Luther King, Jr. said, "*You don't have to see the whole staircase. Just take the first step.*"[36] Help your kids figure out how they can handle each fear, and then come up with a plan. Asa, our 9-year-old grandson, was afraid to join any sports team for a few years. His parents had signed him up for a recreational soccer team; but he sat on the sideline — with his head down — and refused to go in. Yet he loved to play soccer at home, where we clearly saw his athleticism and love of the sport. After figuring out that his fear had to do with not being sure what to do once he was out on the field, they invited a soccer coach to come to their home and give him a lesson. This step broke the resistance, and today Asa plays on a select team and can't wait for the games. He simply needed the safe experience of working with an official coach on his home turf. Not only does he want to join soccer teams, but he begs to play all the other ball sports as well.

Identifying the fear and the root cause helps set up an effective plan. An important step in any plan you set up is to share Biblical truths for your kids to ponder as they work through their worries. Teach them: "*Every tomorrow has two handles. We can take hold of it with the handle of anxiety or the handle of faith.*[37] (Henry Ward Beecher) Here are some Scriptures to share with them:

- God's love for them does not rise and fall with their behavior or performance. (Romans 5:8)

- They are good enough because of what Christ did for them. (Romans 6:23)

- The fear of man lays a snare, but whoever trusts in the Lord is safe. (Proverbs 29:25)

- They can do all things through Him who strengthens them. (Philippians 4:13)

- Philippians 4:4-7, Matthew 6:24, 1 Peter 5:7, Psalm 23:4, Psalm 118:6

TIP 2: "What is the worst-case scenario?"

As Hadassah was preparing to perform at a major Irish dance competition, she began to grow anxious. As she held her churning tummy, with tears running down her cheeks, I sat down beside her and asked, *"What is the worst thing that can happen as you perform?"* She answered, *"I fall down, get hurt and embarrass myself."* Then I asked her if she could get through that to which she replied with a smile, *"I guess I could!"*

Once a child can define the worst-case scenario, their anxiety seems to settle. It does for me, too. Part of gaining a handle on stress is to realize that we will be able to handle even the worst-case scenario because we are not alone. God gives us the capacity to handle what happens when it occurs.

TIP 3: Change your focus.

When Erin, my oldest daughter, was a third grader, she began coming home each day with sad tales of how she was treated at school. Wanting to be an attentive mom, I would sit with her on our living room couch, ask her about her day and listen as she tearfully told me of how she was being mistreated. A student pushed her out of line. Another grabbed her lunch. Daily, someone excluded her or made fun of her.

Growing concerned, I turned to my mentor who asked me, "*Could you unintentionally be growing her fears by asking about them and giving them so much attention?*" Then she encouraged me to focus instead on what was going well at school each day and talk about topics that fueled joy. As I changed my focus and what I questioned her about, Erin's attitude shifted as well, and she started sharing good news with me instead. What we pay attention to we will grow!

After Paul exhorted the church in Philippi not to worry but to pray, he went on to tell believers to think on things that are true, honorable, just, pure, lovely, and commendable, excellent and worthy of praise. (Philippians 4:8) Focusing on positive aspects of our lives is an effective way to ease our worries and those of our children.

Setting up a "worry time" can work with young kids who are in a habit of worrying throughout the day. Let them know you have set aside time when they can come talk about the things that they are worried about. This is a time when they can say whatever they want to say about their fears. Your role is to listen first and offer suggestions; but outside this time, let them know there will be no talking about them. In this way, your child can express what they are feeling but also the boundaries and the encouragement not to consume their day – or yours — with worry.

TIP 4: Change your language.

The language of anxiety often seems to permeate conversations. We talk about how busy we are. How overwhelmed and stressed out we feel. We worry that our kids feel overly stressed and unable to face difficult challenges and major disappointments. All this chatter about stress may increase stress, however. We certainly need to be mindful of reducing schedules that routinely are too busy and addressing ways to reduce stress, but our kids will benefit from learning how to manage stressful times occasionally as well. Challenging times provide our children with opportunities to grow resilience. How we talk about and respond to these times will impact how they learn to respond. You can:

- Reframe negative thoughts into more positive or realistic ones.

- Give everyone permission to put a pause on worrying.

- Consider if things are really as bad as you think.

- Interrupt thoughts with prayer, breathing, moving around, exercise.

TIP 5: Live with hope. Give them hope.

When I feel stressed, the scope of what I focus on narrows down to what is bothering me. If I am hit by multiple stressful circumstances all at once, my view becomes even more myopic. If I can widen my view and consider what's beyond my world of stress, my anxiety lessens. It is no different for kids when they begin to feel anxious, so intentionally distract and disrupt their anxious thinking. Bake cookies together. Look through photo books. Go for a bike ride.

If I can take my eyes off worldly things and gaze up at heavenly things, my anxiety dissipates. Hope is the antidote for anxiety. Hope is believing in things not yet seen. We gain hope when we intentionally pursue God with our thoughts instead of just letting our minds run freely. Cultivating hope in our kids is the pathway out of anxiety. Billy Graham said, *"Anxiety is the natural result when our hopes are centered in anything short of God and His will for us."*

TIP 6: A Note to Anxious Parents

To tell a parent not to worry about their children seems improbable. Much of our thinking as parents revolves around how to best care for our children. And we worry when we don't know what to do! Worry is a trust issue. I have carried a great deal of anxiety about my children over the years. I am so grateful for God's Word which has the solution for addressing our anxious thoughts. My go-to passage, paraphrased here, is found in Philippians 4:4-13. If anxiety is an issue for you, I encourage you to press these verses into your heart and recite them when you are tempted to be overcome by anxious thinking. Remember that worry is a real emotion, but it does not have to dictate what you do.

Philippians 4:4-13

- Rejoice — choose joy. Paul emphasizes this truth by repeating it twice!

- Remind yourself that the LORD is here. He is WITH you.

- Do not be anxious about anything! Nothing is too big for God.

- Instead pray with both thanksgiving and with supplication. Gratitude has a way of lifting our spirits by focusing on what we are thankful for. Supplication means to plead earnestly with God, making your requests known to Him.

- The result is an overflowing of God's peace, which surpasses all understanding, that will guard your hearts and minds in Christ Jesus.

THERE's more—

- Turn your thoughts to things that are true, honorable, just, pure, lovely, commendable, excellent and worthy of praise.

- Be content in whatever situation you are in, which is the opposite of anxiety.

- Remember that you can do all things through Him who strengthens you.

THE ANGRY CHILD

*Whoever is slow to anger has great understanding, but he who has
a hasty temper exalts folly.* — Proverbs 14:29

I was raised by a father who had a temper. His anger would flare up
when we messed up. My siblings and I chose to distance ourselves from him
as a result. However, I picked up his temper along the way and struggled
with anger myself as a young mom. Each time I lost my temper with my
children, I felt terribly guilty afterwards and pledged to try harder moving
forward. Breaking this tendency felt impossible to me. Only as I learned to
surrender this bent and allowed the Holy Spirit to have His way in me did
I gain freedom from this cycle of anger. If you or your child has an anger
problem, I pray this section will be an encouragement and help you find
freedom as well from the tight control that anger can hold.

Addressing angry children begins with dealing with your heart. Anger
itself is always a secondary emotion that rears up when triggered by something else. Anger is a means by which we protect ourselves or cover up other
vulnerable emotions. Anger flows out of primary feelings such as:

- Hurt — emotional or physical

- Humiliation or embarrassment

- Rejection

- Frustration

- Guilt

Anger is expressed in two very opposite ways. We either clam up and
shut down, or we blow up. Same with your kids. When we clam up, we
internalize our anger. We do so by withdrawing emotionally, giving a cold
shoulder, sulking or pouting. When we blow up, we vent out anger. We
do this by yelling, name calling, using sharp sarcasm or even resorting to
throwing, hitting and kicking things. Some people develop a cycle of blowing up, then withdrawing until the pressure builds up to a boiling point and

then blowing up again. Neither clamming up nor blowing up are healthy responses. Following are some tips and suggestions that can help your kids deal with their feelings in healthy ways.

TIP 1: Help your children identify and define their feelings.

When we try to dismiss emotions — to get past them quickly, we may be giving our children the impression that emotions are unimportant. When we disapprove of negative emotions, we are saying they need to be squashed. At the same time, when we accept all emotions, we may be failing to help our children establish limits on appropriate behaviors and responses. All children need to gain the ability to understand and recognize their emotions to make wise decisions and deal with anger effectively. Rather than dismiss, disapprove or remain carefree about all emotions, we can value even the negative emotions as invitations to bond and teach our kids how to problem-solve through their big feelings.

TIP 2: Keep your children fed and hydrated.

I read that a vast percentage of meltdowns in children can be related to hunger or thirst. I believe it! The first warning signs that my blood sugar is dropping too low are irritation and anxiety. If I ignore the signs, I soon feel too ill to eat. I didn't understand this as a child, however; and it took me into adulthood to understand my need to eat something nourishing when I began to feel grumpy. Even being slightly dehydrated can cause moodiness, so help your kids get into the habit of maintaining their body's health with regular meals and consistent water intake.

TIP 3: Don't give in to temper tantrums.

At a younger age, my granddaughter Bethlehem would try to get her way with loud, wailing temper tantrums. Trying to get her to stop was impossible. One day she asked me to put her hair into two braids; but when I finished, she decided that one braid would be better. When I declined to redo her hair, she threw a volatile fit. Thinking of how to respond, I pulled out my phone to video her and asked, "*Would you like to see what you look and sound like throwing a fit?*" She screamed even louder, but it didn't take long for the tantrum to wind down and for her to beg me not to send the video to her parents. If I had responded to her demands, I would have given her the satisfaction of knowing she had manipulated me, and she would have tried this method again. Instead she stopped throwing fits about hair styling.

TIP 4: Communicate wisely in a way that does not provoke anger.

Punitive, anger-laced words work temporarily because kids may obey out of fear; but they can harden — rather than soften — a heart. Here are some suggestions on how to communicate in ways that do not provoke anger in our children:

- Use a respectful tone, and do not mock or ridicule.

- Listen attentively to their opinions.

- Remain calm and not agitated. "*A soft answer turns away wrath, but a harsh word stirs up anger*" (Proverbs 15:1, New King James Version).

- Admit when you are wrong.

- Refrain from comparing your kids.

- Do not use manipulative words.

TIP 5: Grow aware of the early warning signs.

I can tell when a grandchild is about to "lose it" during their school days with me. This is more likely to happen when they have made repeated mistakes on math assignments or when an assignment feels too difficult or when they are just needing a break. If I can intercept the fall before it happens, I can prevent the angry outburst from happening. When I sense that a child is about to spin out of control, I encourage them to take a break. A walk outside to breathe. Sitting in a quiet room to pray. When a child is about to explode, their emotions flood their brains and take over their thinking. When that happens, nothing positive will come out of their mouths until they settle down. Taking a break settles their mind and gets them thinking clearly again. Plus, it grows positive coping skills in response to stress. Once they have settled down, the circumstances that triggered their anger can be discussed but never when they are feeling explosive. Wait to teach until anger has dissipated in you as well.

TIP 6: Maintain your authority as parents.

Years ago, I stepped into a mentoring relationship with the mom of an exceedingly angry boy, her only child. As I listened to her talk, I soon learned that their home was very child-centered. Her young son was in the driver's seat, and his opinion was on equal par with his parents. In fact, his opinions ruled. Even in choosing what home to buy, he was given the final say. I am not kidding. This mom's relationship to her son took precedence over all of her other relationships, including her husband. Her son was in charge; and when his demands were not met, he grew angry. He also grew angry at school when he did not get his way. Anger grew as his expectations were unmet — something he had come to believe he deserved from everyone. His mom wanted him to be happy, and she mistakenly assumed that giving in to his demands was the way to achieve this goal.

Yet our goal, as parents, should be about their growth in Christlikeness and not happiness. Temporary happiness is different from true joy, which comes by way of virtuous character and a willingness to consider the needs of others. To that end, parents must remain in a position of authority and influence with their children. While it's good to get input and ideas from all family members, parents should have the final say in decision-making until their children are old enough — and wise enough — to decide for themselves.

On the other hand, as your children mature, grant them increasing decision-making to meet their growing need to be responsible for themselves.

Children grow angry when they have too much say but also when their opinions do not matter. Learning how to decide for themselves is an important skill to learn, so start with unimportant choices when they are little. Then slowly increase their options so that, by the time they leave your home, they are equipped to handle most decisions on their own.

TIP 7: Share Scripture about anger with your children.

Scripture reaches the heart as nothing else can. God's Word is *"...living and active, sharper than any two-edged sword..."* (Hebrews 4:12). Here are some verses to share on anger:

- **James 1:19-20** — "...let every person be quick to hear, slow to speak, slow to anger; for the anger of man does not produce the righteousness of God."

- **Proverbs 14:29** — "Whoever is slow to anger has great understanding, but he who has a hasty temper exalts folly."

- **Proverbs 19:11** — "Good sense makes one slow to anger, and it is his glory to overlook an offense."

- **Proverbs 15:18** — "A hot-tempered man stirs up strife, but he who is slow to anger quiets contention."

THE PERFECTIONIST CHILD

At its root, perfectionism isn't really about a deep love of being meticulous. It's about fear. Fear of making a mistake. Fear of disappointing others. Fear of failure. [38]
— Michael Law, *Fear of Success.*

Some kids (and parents) believe they can be happy only when they achieve perfection. But striving for perfection is a recipe for failure because it is unachievable. We can never be perfect. Some would argue this statement as they read Matthew 5:48. Jesus did say, "*You therefore must be perfect, as your heavenly Father is perfect.*" Consider the meaning of "perfect" in Greek — *to be complete, brought to wholeness or maturity.* It is referring to human integrity and virtue and about becoming complete or whole in Christ. Not perfection in and of themselves.

A perfectionist is a person with a disposition to regard anything short of perfection as unacceptable. Perfectionists realize they can't be perfect in everything, so they choose areas in which to strive. Perfectionists respond in different ways, however. Some are over-achievers who exhaust themselves regularly, doing more than is required. My youngest daughter responded in this way. In Geometry as a 10th grader, she continued to study for the final exam — even though she could have bombed the final and still had an A in the class. That is all because she wanted a perfect score. We made her stop studying and go have some fun with her friends — a healthier option in her case.

Other perfectionists respond by under-achieving. Their greatest fear is to discover that their best effort is not good enough, so to not try feels safer. When they don't try, they can rationalize why their performance is underwhelming. These individuals back away from pressure and prefer to skate under the radar, where they often go unnoticed. Under-achievers act like they don't care and come across as unmotivated, but don't be fooled by their facade. Deep down inside, they care too much to risk trying and failing. Instead they stay in a safety zone, where they can feel OK about achievement but still a frustrating distance from success.

A perfectionist connects being perfect with their self-identity. If they can do something perfectly, they are valuable and worthy of love and respect. If they mess up, their worth drops — a devastating feeling. Perfectionism can have a debilitating effect on athletes who grow overly concerned and anxiety-ridden over mistakes. Perfectionism may be the ultimate self-defeating behavior because it keeps individuals focused on failure and winds up undermining achievement.

We live in a culture that extols perfection. Our kids are exposed to perfect bodies, perfect facts, perfect hair, perfect nails and perfectly white teeth each time they look at the media. Social media portrays perfect lives. Parents long for the perfect home and perfect car. We spend hours searching for perfect clothing. Young athletes set their sights on pro sports, while parents set expectations for top-tier schools for their kids. Perhaps this is why there seems to be growing numbers of kids with this agonizing bent.

Warning Signs

If you are wondering whether you — or your child — is a perfectionist, below are some warning signs. If you think you might have this bend, consider yourself as you read these. Evaluating yourself will help you understand how your child might be feeling:

- You only allow brief elation over high achievement because you move right on to stressing over the next challenge. Instead of joy, you feel relief.

- You don't experience normal disappointment with failure. Instead you experience devastation because failure is an attack on your value as a person.

- You are haunted by uncertainty over your performance, which gets in the way of enjoying life.

- You worry that your mistakes cause others to think badly of you.

- You experience a steady stream of negative emotions — an endless internal report card that keeps you engaged in perpetual self-evaluation.

- You refrain from engaging in challenging experiences when you are uncertain of your skills.

- You procrastinate by putting off doing a task until you have it lined up perfectly.

- You feel envy when someone else rises above you in some things.

- You prefer to conceal mistakes, which prevents you from getting crucial feedback.

It's possible to become a healthy perfectionist. Such a person gains a sense of satisfaction for a job done right. A healthy perfectionist finds joy in their successes and values the accomplishments of others. They have learned how to face challenges with courage and not shrink from them. Whatever they do, they work heartily but not to receive praise from men. (Colossians 3:23) They are validated based on their efforts, and they do not need praise to feel worthy. Following are suggestions for helping your child become a healthy perfectionist and not an unhealthy one:

- Teach your kids that success hinges less on getting everything right and more on how they handle getting things wrong. This is where creativity, passion and perseverance come into play.

- Create safety for your kids to make mistakes and help them regard mistakes as learning opportunities.

- Expect your kids to try activities at which they are not proficient. The only way to move past some fears is to face them head on.

- Focus on improvement, on getting better.

- Focus on attitude over performance and on effort over the final product. Effort is the key to future mastery and success.

- Reward the process and the effort, not the talent or the outcome. If you praise a kid's intelligence, then when they fail at something, they think they are not smart.

- Perfectionists struggle with being evaluated. To make your suggestions more palatable, refrain from giving your evaluation before you have allowed your child to evaluate themselves. They will be much more receptive to hearing what you have to say after you have allowed them to evaluate their work and what they think they could do better.

- Give up your right to be right. Admit your mistakes, and model a teachable spirit.

- Refuse to respond to failure by getting angry or resentful or giving a "cold shoulder." Help them understand that your love for them is not contingent on their performance.

- Focus on telling your children what you want them to do instead of what they did wrong.

- Be careful with material rewards for performance, which can kill internal motivation by turning an activity into pressured work.

THE DISHONEST CHILD

Whoever walks in integrity will be delivered, but he who is crooked in his ways will suddenly fall.

Proverbs 28:18

When a child lies, it feels like betrayal, leaving the parent frustrated, angry and in a battle to gain an admission of dishonesty. Plus, it's discouraging because we know what the Bible says about lying:

- "Lying lips are an abomination to the LORD..." (Proverbs 12:22).

- "Do not lie to one another..." (Colossians 3:9).

- "...the LORD hates a lying tongue..." (Proverbs 6:16-17).

- "No one who practices deceit shall dwell in my house..." (Psalm 101:7).

Clearly, lying is a moral issue that needs to be addressed; but to address it wisely, we also must consider the reasons why kids lie in the first place. Very, very few kids lie for no reason; and even though the reason is wrong, they may choose to lie anyway. Understanding what motivates a child to lie is not about excusing the behavior but about discerning what drives a child to do so. Inner desires will drive behaviors because our hearts follow what we treasure. (Matthew 6:21) When dishonesty results in gaining what a child wants, then lying becomes the chosen course of action. So get to the heart of why your child may be driven to lie in the first place. Here are a few reasons:

TIP 1: Young kids can have wild imaginations.

It's important to note that young children can struggle to distinguish between imaginative play and reality. I get a kick out of listening to my youngest granddaughter Beth when she is playing with her dolls. Pretending she is one of them, she argues, advises and then goes on to resolve the issues. This type of play builds problem-solving skills — even though none of it is real or true, except to Beth, who fully immerses herself in the pretend drama. As a young child, my oldest daughter Erin would describe various outlandish experiences, which we came to realize were episodes of her imagination seeping into her real world.

A four-year-old preschool student once told me that he was there in Israel when Jesus got nailed to the cross. No amount of explaining how impossible that was could persuade him otherwise. He was convinced he had been present. And somewhere in a dream or an imaginative play, he had been! These are not lies or an intent to deceive but a child who still lacks the awareness that what he is experiencing is not real.

TIP 2: Kids lie to problem-solve and to avoid trouble.

Lying is an immature way in which kids choose to deal with a problem they are facing and avoid trouble or an angry response from someone. Your daughter may forget to do a homework assignment. Rather than admit the omission, she chooses to blame the teacher for losing her paper to avoid the consequences. Or your teenager chooses to stay out later than agreed upon but blames a traffic jam or wreck for his tardiness to avoid the punishment. Help your child understand that this means of solving their problem is wrong and then guide them into considering wiser problem-solving methods — perhaps by choosing well to begin with.

TIP 3: Kids lie to not disappoint or hurt others.

Some children lie because they worry that the truth will disappoint others, especially those who have a people-pleasing bent to their personalities. Your daughter really doesn't like her best friend's new shoes, but she tells her they are adorable. Your son will never wear the sweater Grandma sent him although he has told her how much he likes it. Of course, we don't want our children to hurt others with thoughtless statements, but we also need to be mindful of not justifying dishonesty.

Some kids will choose to lie by inflating or exaggerating their achievements to not disappoint loved ones. Another related reason kids may lie — especially in the adolescent and teen years — is that they are afraid to reveal their true feelings about stressful challenges they are facing. They choose instead to be dishonest about something that may feel embarrassing to them.

TIP 4: Kids lie to gain an advantage or control over others.

Proving your child has lied is a messy trap in which you don't want to get stuck. "*Try to prove I lied*" is a struggle for power you need to avoid because it gives the child control in which he or she may actually enjoy getting you caught. In this case, lying is about gaining an advantage or control over you. If this is your child, let him or her know that you have the right to choose — based on their past behavior — whether to believe them or not. If they are being honest, then it's your burden to bear; but if they are choosing to not come clean, you feel sad for them. No arguing. No lecturing. Don't fuel their need to demonstrate power in this manner by jumping into a tug-of-war, which no one can win.

TIP 5: Kids lie to gain an independent identity.

My sister Kathy took mascara and lipstick to school in seventh grade although our parents had forbidden it. She would arrive home and run into the bathroom to remove her makeup before our parents would notice. Her desire to identify with a certain group of girls at school was stronger than her desire to obey Mom and Dad. In her case, lying about the makeup was an attempt to gain independence and separation as an individual. Plus, she was trying to boost her self-esteem. Wearing makeup was more important to her than honesty. She was trying to construct things in the way she wanted them to be.

What can parents do to address dishonesty in an effective manner that leads to heart change? Here are a few suggestions that will guide your efforts.

TIP 6: Address the underlying behavior.

Once you discern the underlying reason your child might lie, consider how to deal with the underlying behavior. For example, guide your daughter to gain the skills and habits that will help her turn in all her homework on time. Work out a plan by which your teen can appeal for a later curfew, when appropriate, so that he will be less tempted to lie. Consider your daughter's desire to look pretty when you establish rules about makeup and dress. Address your children's growing need for independence as they age by slowly increasing what they are responsible for — as well as allowing them more decision-making — when they show the maturity to do so.

TIP 7: Don't react immediately.

When you catch your child in a serious lie that makes you want to throttle him or her, don't react immediately. Calm down. Pray. Talk with your spouse, family member or a trusted friend. When you respond impulsively — without thought or prayer, chances are you will hand out an over-the-top punishment you later regret. Remember not to argue about the lie; just state what is obvious. Concentrate on listening so that you hear what occurred that made your child feel the need to lie. Because lying is often the way your child is trying to problem-solve, make sure to listen to your child explain. This will give you insights as to the motivation for lying and make a safe place where your child can open up and talk about what is really going on.

TIP 8: Discern whether the lie was an impulsive reaction or a pondered deception.

My grandson will forget to put his bike away properly. When confronted, he will quickly spout, *"Not me! I put it away in the right spot."* If pushed aggressively, he will dig in stubbornly and insist that he is not lying. However, if he is given a second chance immediately with a response from me like: *"I bet you want to take that back, and give me an honest answer instead,"* he is far more apt to confess. His on-the-spot solution to a problem is denial, but then he is stuck having to defend a lie as well. Often we can forgo a bigger conflict in these types of situations by simply discerning whether the lie was childish impulsivity or pondered deception, which should be dealt with differently.

TIP 9: Consider additional consequences for lying.

When children lie, it's tempting to respond in angry, punitive ways because we deeply value integrity. But angry punishment does little to reach the heart. Plus, we often wind up regretting these over-the-top punishments when we cool down. You simply will NOT be able to punish your child into virtuous choices. An aggressive approach just ends up in a power struggle, with kids digging in their heels deeper and distancing themselves from you further.

Natural or logical consequences are impactful because they place the ownership of the misbehavior on the child. When a child lies about something they did wrong, additional consequences are in order. These consequences should hurt enough that the child comes to prefer honesty over what he is trying to gain by lying. When admitting their wrongdoing results in lesser consequences than lying about it, they are more apt to break the habit of lying.

There are many reasons why kids lie, and the key is to understand the underlying motivations and address the issue at the heart level. They already know lying is wrong — we just need to get them to see it as undesirable.

THE ARGUMENTATIVE CHILD

> *A fool gives full vent to his spirit, but a wise man quietly holds it back.*
>
> Proverbs 29:11

Proverbs 8:33 tells us to *"hear instruction and be wise, and do not neglect it"*; but receiving correction is not an easy pill to swallow. Who enjoys having their mistakes pointed out? Like us, our children have an intense need to be right; so when a wrong is pointed out, they are likely to argue instead of humbly receiving it. I face this on a regular basis when teaching my grandkids, who genuinely want their math answers to be correct and their writing to be without flaws.

Arguing does have its merits, however. We certainly want our children to communicate their thoughts and to stand up for what they believe. By arguing, kids often are trying to present their ideas and express their opinions; but they haven't yet learned how to do so without being disrespectful or offending others. As an adolescent or a teen, they may press in even harder as they form their opinions. This is a very normal stage in which they are trying to develop their interests and ideas and how to express them.

To be able to receive corrections without getting defensive and arguing is important, however. Not only does it indicate a growth in humility, but kids who argue too much also are being disrespectful. Some kids will begin to argue — even before they have listened to what their parents have to say because it has become a habit. Some kids habitually share their opinions — whether they know what they are talking about or not. They try to drown out everyone else around them, which can be annoying for others. Following are some TIPS on dealing with argumentative children.

TIP 1: Be silent.

It's hard — very hard — but try to be silent when you find yourself in an argument with your son or daughter. An argument only happens when you let one take place, so choose to not argue. With your have-to-be-right kid, try not responding to them when they try to engage you in an argument. Each time you respond, they feel compelled to answer, and the argument keeps going in a louder and more hostile direction.

TIP 2: Listen attentively ONE time.

You will glean valuable insights when you listen attentively to your child's point of view. Teens can be intense — and even obnoxious in expressing their opinions, especially during the stage when they are trying to separate who they are from who their parents think they should be. Something important may be revealed as they express themselves; so listen to the underlying sentiments, and prayerfully try to discern what is fueling your son or daughter's opinions.

However, listen once. Make it clear that they are allowed to state their opinion one time to you. In return, you will state your opinion once as well. Everyone's opinion is valued. **One time.** When stated over and over, it becomes badgering and pestering. Don't respond defensively or take their opinions personally; and don't be frightened or threatened by them either. Your children, especially the pre-teens and teens, are in the process of shaping their opinions; and what they say is far less important than what their behavior tells you.

It's this simple: Listen. State your opinion. Let them respond. Then respectfully pull out of the conversation.

TIP 3: Use few words — ask questions instead.

Parents often feel like they must get the last word as the authority, and the child feels they must as well to maintain control. It's a power struggle in which no one wins. Plus, kids think if they just explain a bit better — or with more force — that their parents will accept what they have to say. Staying in an argument with your kids strengthens arguing. As they develop their personal and social lives, they desire more power and control. After you have listened to an opinion of theirs with which you disagree, respond with something like: *"I hear you and get how you feel, but this is how it's going to be."* Use as few words as possible; and maintain a calm, clear look on your face. Then walk away. Your son or daughter needs to know that your family does not operate merely around his or her opinion and that — while you will listen and consider their ideas — you are the parent and, as such, you have the final say.

In addition, think of good questions to ask them — one that will make them think. *"How is this going to work out for you?"* *"What will you do differently next time?"* The standard answer to probing questions, which stubborn kids like to give is: *"I don't know!"* If your child tries this approach with you, respond back with something like: *"If you could think of an answer, what would it be?"* or *"If you were able to do the right thing, what do you think you would do?"*

TIP 4: Disagree respectfully.

Last week, when I told my 9-year-old grandson that I would not listen to arguing, he yelled, *"I am not arguing! I am telling!"* Later when things cooled down, I explained how he would be far more likely to get a positive response if he chose to share his opinion or state his request respectfully.

More disrespectful than arguing is to silently ignore what a parent says, however. By arguing, a child is acknowledging that parents have the right to set limits and make demands, and they exercise their growing need to govern their lives. The key is learning how to use reasoned words and not angry yelling to settle a difference. While parents should have the ultimate say, especially in important decisions, trying to understand the child's perspective will help pave the way for respectful discussions. You don't have to agree to understand! *"A fool takes no pleasure in understanding, but only in expressing his opinion"* (Proverbs 18:2).

TIP 5: Evaluate how you communicate.

Positive, affirming comments should always greatly outweigh your negative comments. In fact, nagging and lecturing reinforce a child's need to argue. In addition, correction is far more effective than criticism. Correction is telling your child what you want them to do. Criticism is telling them what they have done wrong. The former is forward-looking, and the latter is about what has occurred already.

"Speak calmly" versus *"stop shouting."*

"Put your clothes where they belong" versus *"quit leaving your clothes on the floor."*

Build trust by saying what you mean and meaning what you say – however, not in a mean way. According to Michel de Montaigne, a French philosopher in the 1500s, *"He who establishes his argument by noise and command shows that his reason is weak."*[39] Speak respectfully to your children, limiting your words to what is necessary because they will tune out any lengthy, nagging lecture.

TIP 6: Don't be the referee.

What is it about arguing that kids enjoy? My grandkids will pretend to argue — even when they have nothing to argue about! If you have more than one child, you likely experience sibling arguments on a regular basis as well. One very important key is not to get in the habit of stepping in as the referee. Trying to determine who is at fault is a "lose-lose" proposition for you. One child will be smug and happy, and the other will be sullen and angry. Sometimes you have no choice because the offense is so egregious and obvious. However, whenever possible, let your kids solve their problems and work out their disagreements. Stepping in takes away their learning opportunity; and furthermore, it becomes a means by which your kids control your time. They quickly learn that tattling draws you in.

My grandkids often behave more like siblings because they spend a great deal of time together. When they have a disagreement while out playing soccer or basketball, I expect them to work out their issue before coming to me. When they do come to me, I expect the same conclusion from all parties. They are expected to agree upon what took place and doing so requires coming to a truthful conclusion. Sometimes they simply see what happened from different perspectives; and at those times, I still expect them to find common ground in agreeing to disagree.

Finally, spending time together should be considered a privilege — one that is earned by being pleasant to be around. When arguments happen that upset others and make the entire home feel like a battle zone, separation may be the best solution for a while. It will bring peace to the parents and time to unwind for the kids. Arguing does not need to defile the culture of your home.

CHAPTER SIX

Lies Students Believe –

and the Truth They Need Instead

"Knowing who you are in Christ will transform your life like nothing else." [40]

—Neil T. Anderson

Lies our children are persuaded to believe lead them into troubling behaviors. Deception has always been the tactic of the father of lies, who *"prowls around like a roaring lion, seeking someone to devour"* (1 Peter 5:8). Without a doubt, he is after your boys and girls; and he knows that deceptive ideas — formed in their minds — will lead to poor behavior and destructive decisions. The student ministry division of Neil T. Anderson's Freedom in Christ Ministries lists three big lies students fall for, which I wish to expand on here. Uncovering these lies and guiding our children to replace them with God's truth are imperative as we disciple their hearts.

LIE: Great accomplishments will make me feel accepted and valued.

Our youngest daughter Alisa was an outstanding swimmer. Growing up, she won numerous state awards; and as a 14-year-old, she landed a spot on the National Junior Team. As a junior in high school, she qualified for the Olympic Trials. She was heavily recruited by colleges and chose to swim for The University of Texas. In her freshman year, she broke the Big 12 conference record in the 400 Individual Medley. Just a few months later, however, her performance began to flounder. The harder she tried, the worse her times became. Not only did she struggle in the water, but she began to struggle emotionally and mentally as well. Nothing felt right, and she fell into a lengthy depression. If she couldn't swim well, who was she and what did she have to offer?

Months later, doctors determined that she had been swimming with mononucleosis. As she began to recover, the illness came back with vengeance — likely because she had not taken time off to rest. This trend resulted in a second season during which Alisa was unable to perform at the level expected of a scholarship swimmer, which was exceedingly difficult for someone who had come to see her identity and worth largely in swimming. If she was unable to swim well enough to score points for the team, what value was she to the swim program who was paying for her education?

Thankfully, her coaches saw something more in her and selected her to be the team captain. They wisely reminded her that swimming was simply going back and forth in the water and not what defined her. God used her coaches — and a devoted campus minister from her church — to strip off the deceptive lies that had been governing her thinking. The Lord used illness to transform her identity back to Him. While she remains a very driven and competitive person, this experience, which felt utterly devastating at the time, has grown her into a mom who wisely guides her four children — all who are competitors by nature.

Athletic stardom will fade in time. It always does. Athletes often struggle when the fading occurs — perhaps because of a lack of identity outside their success. Being a superstar athlete is not a bad thing in and of itself; but if your child is one, here are a few thoughts to keep in mind:

- Make sure to teach him or her that their lasting acceptance and value do not lie in their performance but in Jesus alone. Knowing who you are in Jesus is an identity that will never fade.

- Focus on attitudes and not accomplishments.

- Affirm them for how they behave and not for how they perform.

LIE: Good looks — plus admiration of others — will make me feel secure.

Adolescents often face strong pressure to meet cultural standards with their appearance. This quest for the perfect look and shape can take a harmful toll on a child's confidence and health. They long for the admiration of peers as a means by which they can fit in and belong. The rise in disordered eating is just one of the debilitating outcomes when adolescents form unhealthy assumptions about their appearance. Eating disorders are now the third most common chronic illness among female teenagers, and they represent the highest mortality rate of any mental illness.

You might assume that Camille, a thin 15-year-old girl with a lovely face and beautiful hair, feels better about herself than her short, stocky friend whose frizzy hair is hard to manage and whose acne is impossible to hide. According to a study published recently in *The Journal of Clinical Child and Adolescent Psychology*,[42] beauty and self-esteem do not actually go together, however. Instead this study indicated that adolescents, who were assessed with lower levels of self-esteem, often were rated as most attractive compared to their peers. Why would attractiveness harm one's self-esteem? Perhaps it's because being considered attractive by others sets up the expectation to maintain the look. How can I keep this look up day after day? Plus, if appearance becomes the goal, there's always someone with nicer clothes and better looks. The chase never ends, and the standard keeps changing. What can parents do?

- Emphasize an inner beauty formed by character. Be mindful of what you comment on.

- Guide them to spend more time doing what they enjoy doing and developing their talents.

- Do your best to limit and oversee their social media activity.

Social media continually exposes our children to images of "perfect" body types, moving them to compare themselves to others. They can easily form unrealistic ideals for themselves based on what they see and then feel distressed when they are unable to meet these ideals. The more your child compares himself or herself to others – and social media heightens comparison, the more concerned they grow over their body image.

LIE: Status and popularity — plus recognition from others — will make me feel significant.

Over the years spent working in school settings, I have watched a predictable social pattern emerge that often reaches a peak in seventh and eighth grades. This pattern has to do with the emergence of a group of kids who label themselves as the "popular ones." The composition of this group includes a leader who determines the rules of behavior necessary to be accepted, the followers who do what it takes to remain in the group and the "wannabes" who long to get in. Usually, these so-called rules include the requirement to only associate with those who have been deemed as acceptable and to exclude everyone else. This pattern creates a great deal of social anxiety — especially for the "wannabes" whose emotions are on a roller-coaster ride, with acceptance being granted one day and removed the next. Thankfully, there's always a group of kids who do not get caught up in this social engineering; and they are usually the largest group.

Ironically, this so-called popular group is often not broadly well-regarded — except by themselves. Not only do they strive to maintain control, but they crave the attention that comes with being in this group. This perceived popularity is more about staying in control and less about being a good friend. The leaders may act confident but have a deep need to remain in the driver's seat — likely out of deep insecurities. Here are some tips on how to guide your kids through the inherent social challenges they face in these years:

- If your child is one of the students in this 'popular" group, be especially mindful to emphasize kindness, inclusivity and compassion towards others. Refrain from encouraging social engagements solely within this group.

- Talk to your children about what makes a good friend; someone who makes them a better version of themselves, who encourages good character and behavior, who is trustworthy. Remind them of the truth in Proverbs 13:20: *"Whoever walks with the wise becomes wise, but the companion of fools will suffer harm."*

- Point out that fear motivates kids to give in to peer pressure – fear of rejection, fear of feeling insignificant, fear of being made fun of. Talk about Proverbs 29:25 which says, *"The fear of man lays a snare, but whoever trusts in the LORD is safe."*

- Teach them to not give up control by acquiescing to the demands of their peers. Social manipulation cannot take place unless your child allows it. Teach them the value of saying "NO" – to not consent when others entice them. (Proverbs 1:10)

- Teach them to stand up for others who are being treated poorly. The so-called "popular" group can tend to operate in a form of social bullying that treats those outside their group in demeaning ways.

Seeking to be popular will never result in the security for which your child longs. Plus, it can lead to poor choices made solely for trying to fit in. The more control your child grants to the demands of social groups, the more prone he or she will be to making choices demanded by this group. Learning how to stand up to social pressures is an important step in maturing. The earlier your child learns how to stand strong against these demands, the more secure he or she will grow.

Replacing the lies with truth.

These three lies have become even more accentuated with the release of the iPhone in 2007, which is now considered a necessity at a younger and younger age. While the iPhone is a great tool, it also can be a constant source of distraction and deception, grabbing one's attention from what is true, good and beautiful. What your children pay attention to ultimately will shape their feelings, which they like to rely on to determine what is real and true to them. While emotions are real, they often fall short of reflecting reality. They provide insights and add vitality to our lives, but they should not rule the day. When emotions become coupled with truth, our children will learn to walk both wisely yet intimately with God and others.

These three lies form faulty attempts to define one's identity – through accomplishments, through admirable appearance and through recognition from others. All three must be replaced by the one transformative truth — that only in Jesus will they find lasting acceptance, security and significance. As Neil T. Anderson said, *"Understanding your identity in Christ is absolutely essential for your success at living a victorious Christian life."* [41]

First and foremost, make sure to regularly point your children to the Gospel. Once they receive Jesus as their Lord and Savior, Biblical truth about their identity will resonate and grant them the acceptance, security and significance they crave. When such truths are pressed into their hearts, there will be little room for deceptive lies to take root:

- I am a child of God. John 1:12

- I have been justified. Romans 5:1

- I have been redeemed and forgiven. Colossians 1:14

- I am complete in Christ. Colossians 2:10

- I am free from condemnation. Romans 8:1-2

- I cannot be separated from the love of God. Romans 8:35-39

- I am hidden with Christ in God. Colossians 3:3

- I have not been given a spirit of fear but of power, love and self-control. 2 Timothy 1:7

- I am born of God; the evil one cannot touch me. 1 John 5:18

- I have been chosen and appointed to bear fruit. John 15:16

- I am God's workmanship. Ephesians 2:10

- I have boldness and may approach God with confidence. Ephesians 3:12

- I can do all things through Christ who strengthens me. Philippians 4:13

CHAPTER SEVEN

TIPS for Teaching at Home

There is no doubt that it is around the family and the home that all the greatest virtues, the most dominating virtues of humans, are created, strengthened and maintained."[43]

—Winston S. Churchill

Since the 2013-14 school year, when I first started teaching each of my grandkids during one of their school days at home each week, I calculated that I have led my 11 grandkids through at least 50 years of grades combined. I started out thinking I would serve as a co-teacher for one year to gain some experience and insights to share with parents. Today, I am still at it; and serving in this role has become my top priority.

The first year was the toughest. I remember facing the day with some trepidation, and that was with only three grandkids! Now, with an additional day each week with more grandkids, I find these days to be an enjoyable challenge. It's certainly challenging, hard work; but it's filled with purpose. Following are the 10 most effective TIPS I have gleaned in this role over the years.

TIP 1: Have a plan with a schedule.

A frustrated mom of five called me one day to tell me she needed to stop teaching her kids at home. "*These days leave me so frazzled and angry, and they really don't want to listen to me anyway,"* she lamented. Undoubtedly, this model is especially difficult for families with multiple young children. This family had enrolled children in kindergarten, second grade and fourth grade. In addition, 18-month-old twins added to the complexity of her days. As we talked on the phone, I asked her how she scheduled her school days at home. *"Schedule?"* she asked. *"I just try to fit school in whenever it works."*

Establishing a plan and a schedule is the first TIP listed because this suggestion alone can make all the difference. It did for this mom. With a little bit of guidance, she quickly devised a schedule suitable for her family's needs. Instead of leaving our school, this family is thriving in our model. To be sure, the days are still hard; but they have become manageable and much more fruitful.

Why form a schedule? *If you fail to plan, you plan to fail* certainly rings true for these school days at home. A schedule provides a bit of control to a day that can fall apart easily. Plus, it establishes priorities. Taking a come-what-may approach — especially with multiple young kids — will leave you feeling exasperated and discouraged. Everyone benefits from some planning and scheduling.

Your schedule need not be rigid but one that forms a relatively consistent structure — yet with plenty of flexibility. I recommend starting and ending your school days at home around a similar time frame as the campus school day — if possible. Most kids function best with a consistent rhythm to their days, which helps them stay more focused. In addition, a predictable structure alleviates anxiety by helping kids know what to expect, which provides a sense of control both for them and you.

While a consistent schedule has many benefits, creative solutions also can make the school day at home more manageable. Some families opt to move certain assignments to the evening before, or they move projects to the weekends. I often ask a grandchild or two to come early (they live next door!) so that my husband can help them with their math homework before the rest arrive. The car is a great place to practice memory work, listen to audible books or quiz your kids on key concepts. The dinner table is a great time to discuss what they are learning in discipleship classes. If both parents work in your household, even greater creativity will be required to set up an effective schedule, with both Mom and Dad involved in the process.

Also, make sure to let your children know that you will be available until a certain time of day — after which they will be on their own to finish any incomplete work. Teach them to take advantage of the time you have granted them and not to waste your time — or theirs. Having the school portion of these days drag on is not healthy for you, your kids or your family. Establishing a schedule with a start and an end time — yet with a bit of wiggle room — will go a long way to protect your time and your energy! The secrets behind success for your days are prayer and a planned agenda!

Sample schedule

How parents schedule school days at home will vary — based on the unique needs and demands of each family. Babies must be fed and attended to. Careers responsibilities must be addressed. Some families teach their young children while also caring for aging parents. Having multiple students in various grades provides a challenge as well. That is my experience with five to six kids at a time in a variety of grades. If God has called you to this model of education, however, there will be a way to manage successfully. Over the years, I have landed on a schedule that works well for me with five to six grandkids at a time. Hopefully, you will be able to glean ideas for yourself as you read this section.

Just as the classroom days are broken into sections, I divide my school day at home into sections as well. I have landed on what I call *Morning Moments* to start the day out — followed by three work sessions, then assignments that are conducted around the snack and lunch table. Prior to each work session, I discuss expectations individually with each child as well as identify the lessons with which they will need guidance and those they can be working on independently while I am busy with others. These work sessions create built-in deadlines and promote efficiency. If you are like me, you work most effectively when time is a bit tight. With endless time to complete an assignment, I tend to procrastinate and waste time. At the end of each session, hardworking grandkids are rewarded with a break; but anyone who chooses to be inefficient gains a shorter break. They all need a break, however, to focus effectively. This structure grows effective habits in my grandkids because it fosters individual responsibility — with accountability along with efficient time-management habits.

As the children age, I allow greater and greater choice in what assignments they do and when — except for math, which I routinely expect to be completed and corrected during the first work session. As long as they are responsible, they are granted increasing freedom. The opposite is also true because I want them to learn that freedom comes with responsible behavior and that freedom is restricted with irresponsible choices.

I encourage you to put together a schedule that meets the needs of your family and that is built around the unique scheduling needs of your children. I always plan for lunch and snack times before the week begins so that I have the ingredients in place. I keep it simple and cycle a few items that have proven to work well with my grandkids. Here's a glimpse of what a day can look like in my home classroom.

- 8:30-8:45 – Morning Moments: Bible lesson, character goals, what to expect in the day, prayer

- 8:45-10 — Work Session 1: Everyone starts with mathematics and begins another subject as time allows.

- 10-10:20 – Break: outdoors whenever possible; indoors during inclement weather but NO SCREENS

- 10:20-10:45 – Snack together around the kitchen table: We do memory work, Scripture memory and any recitations together.

- 10:45-12:15 – Work Session 2: Reading, grammar, writing and/or spelling

- 12:15-1 — Lunch & Break: Read-aloud books or common reading assignments with young kids

- 1-3 — Work Session 3: Any incomplete assignments and projects (older kids may go longer)

At the end of the day, I ask each child how they would evaluate their effort and behavior and then discuss what went well and what to do better the next time. I have concluded that each day needs a launch and closure. I launch the day with *Morning Moments;* and I close with an open, honest evaluation of the day. Teaching your children can be challenging and exhausting, but the benefits are worth it. As the saying goes, days can feel long; yet the years fly by quickly. Teaching young students is most challenging; yet as they advance in grades, they grow more and more independent. This season of life will be over before you know it. I find that my grandkids are harder on themselves than I would be, so I am usually able to zip up even a difficult day with a positive message of how to move forward.

TIP 2: Be prepared.

Years ago, I read John Maxwell's book, *Today Matters,* [45] and gained many insights from his masterful book. One that stands out has to do with daily preparation. He wrote that everyone chooses how to approach life. "If you are proactive, you focus on ***preparing***. If you're reactive, you end up focusing on ***repairing***." This concept is invaluable for the school day at home — really for any day! For example, when I prepare in advance for the school day, I can focus on my grandkids when the day starts. However, if I choose to not be prepared, my time is consumed with a focus on what already should have been done — things like looking over the plans in advance, gathering supplies, etc. In that scenario, I am forced to repair what already should have been accomplished rather than wholly engage in what I should be doing; and the outcome is disorder and ineffectiveness. Being prepared gives me a sense of what the day holds as well as what materials are needed. Plus, it helps me decide who to help during each session and who can work independently. This will allow me to enter the day less frantic, more joyful and able to wholly engage.

TIP 3: Have an efficient set-up and take-down strategy.

This past summer, 8-year-old Alma organized my school supplies and wrote out a list of what supplies needed to be replenished. Then we went shopping together to purchase what was on her list. Later at home, I let her determine how to organize them. She now can help her siblings and cousins find what they need.

When I first began to teach my grandkids, I used to set up the home satellite classroom each day before they arrived and then took it down afterwards. Not anymore! I make sure that I start out the school year with plenty of supplies and materials that are organized in a way that my grandkids know where to find them and put them away. I purchase containers that fit these purposes. For example, one round container has four sections that hold pens, pencils, colored pencils and markers. Another container has scissors and glue. Trays hold an assortment of paper to include lined paper, graph paper, writing sheets and construction paper. Having a solid inventory of supplies goes a long way in saving time and last-minute trips to the store. The children inform me when certain items are running out. Together, we are working on operating in an efficient manner.

TIP 4: Be wholeheartedly and restfully engaged.

Model to your kids that this time with them matters. These opportunities will be over sooner than you think! Multi-task them as little as possible. Put your phone away. As you form your "to-do list," also establish a not-to-do list! What are the things you will not be doing during the school time at home? I put a big X into my planner for each school day at home with my grandkids; and unless it is necessary, I don't allow other requests or opportunities to take away from this time. I know that they will be engaged to the degree that I am.

I recognize that many of you reading this book have limited time because of careers and that your schedule of teaching at home must work around job demands. If God has called you to this model — even though it is hard, stick with it. Your hands-on role will lessen as your child gains the skills for self-directed learning. I urge you to make this time a priority and figure out creative ways to include time in your schedule when you can focus on your role as their teacher. The greatest gift you can give your kids is the feeling that, during these times, nothing else matters more than being fully with them. While these days often hold what feels like a daunting list of to-dos, I remind myself not to make checking off this list my primary aim. These days hold much value when we view them with high value — and the greatest gains lie in our relationships with our children as we guide their character and spiritual formation.

Intentionally focus on the process and not the outcomes. For one grandchild, I may be looking for attention to detail; while for another, I expect better efficiency and not getting lost in detail. With one grandson, I spent a full school year challenging him to respond well to correction; and with a granddaughter, I challenged her to not overreact and fall apart because of mistakes. Character growth takes time; yet when we focus on the skills of learning and attitudes that promote learning, their academic growth takes off. Teaching kids at home is much, much more than merely getting through a checklist.

My mom was always in a hurry. She struggled to enjoy the moment because she was always looking forward to what was next. She was driven to arrive at a future point on her agenda. Sadly, this habit robbed her of the ability to enjoy each day. I see this same tendency in my thinking and have challenged myself to overcome this trait. I am convicted deeply when I read Psalm 39:4-5:

"O LORD, make me know my end

and what is the measure of my days;

let me know how fleeting I am!

Behold, you have made my days a few handbreadths,

and my lifetime is as nothing before you.

Surely all mankind stands as a mere breath!" Selah

I know firsthand how taxing these school days at home can be, but I also know how quickly they pass. Each day can feel like it will never end. Yet the school year will fly by, so take *hurry* out of your daily thought process. While the school day does need to end at a reasonable hour, an inner state of *hurry* robs us of the beauty God has placed before us and of the ability to be gracious to those around us. We need to be able to stop and do what are most important — to pray with a discouraged child. To address conflict wisely. To listen. To seek to understand. Getting things done brings about short-term relief, but getting the right things done ushers in peace. Teaching from a state of rest doesn't mean we stop working but that we cease striving inwardly.

TIP 5: Establish individual goals for each child.

Together with the kids, I establish yearly and daily goals. They vary with each child who each comes with their unique strengths and weaknesses. We discuss these goals openly in front of each other because I want them to know how we are all learning and growing in unique ways. Alma and Asa work on the same math assignment; but Asa needs to learn to slow down and read the directions, while Alma needs to trust her reasoning and just get the assignment done. Hadassah needs to see mistakes as learning opportunities and not failure, while her cousin Isaac needs to be more concerned with copying problems onto paper correctly. Some need to stop interrupting, while others need to gain a teachable spirit or learn to respond more respectfully.

I look for evidence of growth with these established goals, reminding myself that behaviors to which I pay attention will likely grow. Therefore, I prefer to give more attention to what they are doing well than bark at them when they are struggling. With each grandchild, I strive to deepen their understanding and grasp of the Gospel. This requires that I correct wisely and maintain a culture in which they are held to high standards of behavior in gracious ways that point them to Jesus.

TIP 6: Establish clear expectations.

Most behavioral issues are taken care of when clear expectations are defined and reinforced with clarity. Often it is simply a matter of knowing what you expect. Jesus' Golden Rule stands as the one overarching rule we abide by — treat others as you wish to be treated. This covers most things. Here are a few more targeted expectations:

- Treat each other with respect.
- Help each other when appropriate.
- Work hard so that you have time to play hard.
- Ask for help only after you have tried to figure something out yourself. I help kids who are working themselves.
- Solve your conflicts and issues. You are responsible for yourself.

When conflict arises between two grandkids or siblings — and it does, I expect them to sit outside the classroom area and resolve it between themselves before coming to me. They can tell me what happened once they both arrive at the same conclusion. Usually, they are willing to quickly resolve any issue to join back in. On occasion, they simply can't agree because they each see the conflict from distinctly different perspectives. In that case, I ask them to at least understand each other. Learning how to address conflict openly and graciously is a valuable life skill, and these days at home offer many opportunities to practice. I refrain from becoming the referee whenever possible because it is most often a lose-lose situation and does nothing to grow conflict resolution skills in the children.

TIP 7: Partner with the classroom teacher.

Even on the school days at home, you can rely on the partnership with your child's teacher who can back you up as needed. When a grandchild elects to not do his or her work, I remind them that I will inform the classroom teacher of their choice and that their teacher will address the issue at school with them. This usually does the trick! If you make this threat, make sure to follow up with it so that your children know your word is trustworthy.

TIP 8: Be intentional about character and spiritual transformation.

The transfer of faith is what matters most — even during the busy school day at home, which is why the inclusion of topics related to faith and character are key priorities within each day's agenda. It's tempting to skip — especially on days when the workload is heavy or when it does not check a box; but what you prioritize will influence the priorities of your children. You are their most influential model! I like to begin the day with time together, discussing topics that address character and spiritual transformation. Here are some ideas:

- Consistently teach your children the Good News of the Gospel — that Jesus saves us from our sins! I ask my grandkids — on a regular basis — what it means to be saved. By their answers, I see how easily they fall into thinking that their acceptance with God rests in their behavior. Yet what will change their lives and establish steadfast faith are embracing the foundational truths of our faith that are all about Jesus and not about us.

- Teach your children the attributes of God — both those attributes that are unique to Him and the moral attributes in which we are to grow. My young grandkids enjoyed learning about God's attributes like omnipresent, omnipotent and omniscient, which elevated their view of what God is like. Their faith grows when they learn that God is also immutable and sovereign. Their hearts began to grow less anxious when they heard about God's grace, mercy and love.

- Teach stories about Bible heroes, but make sure to include how these individuals also failed at times. They need to see these Bible stories through the lens of a faithful God who restores humanity and not from a moralistic perspective of people who accomplish great things on their own. David is known as a man after God's own heart, but he failed miserably. Peter is the rock on which the Church was built, but he denied Jesus multiple times. Paul was formerly Saul, a persecutor of Christians before his conversion. Mistakes and failures do not need to define us permanently.

- Build prayer into your day. Begin by exalting God for who He is. Your children need to see Jesus not merely as Someone to whom they can send requests but, first and foremost, as King of Kings and Lord of Lords. An accurate view of who He is will hold up through their struggles and disappointments. A low view of God will fall apart when life does not go the way they expect.

- Include others in these prayers as well, making the well-being of each person a priority for all. My grandkids like to pray, holding hands in a circle after our morning opening and before they begin their schoolwork.

- Praise God for what He is doing in your life with your children and encourage them to express thanksgiving as well. We enter into His gates with thanksgiving and with praise. (Psalm 100:4)

- Encourage and allow time for questions about faith. Address concerns as they arise. Share Scripture for them to ponder in response to concerns.

- Make sure they understand the words in Scripture that they are memorizing by asking them about the meaning of the words.

TIP 9: Teaching multiple kids.

This tip is for those of you with larger families who are teaching multiple kids at once — or those of you with a toddler(s) under foot as you attempt to teach your school-age children. Remind yourself that this time will pass, and soon your little ones will not be little anymore. You are in a taxing season and may need to adjust some of your expectations. You will not be able to accomplish all that your friend with one or two children can do. Extra enrichment assignments will likely not get done. It's OK! Your child's projects may not measure up to others. Again, it's OK! Do what you can do and remind yourself of the many wonderful benefits of having a larger family!

These bits of advice helped my daughter Alisa whose days are finally beginning to feel more manageable with one in seventh grade, two in third grade and her youngest in first grade. She sees the light at the end of the tunnel. While the days behind her were difficult, she also looks back and appreciates the journey.

TIP 10: Ask for help.

Teaching kids in this model is hard work, but you need not do it alone. Don't be afraid to ask for help with the challenges you encounter. Do you have a difficult child who exhausts your patience each day or one who refuses to work? Do you need ideas for how to structure your school day? Are you going through a difficult season and simply need someone to pray with you and encourage you? School leaders, ministry personnel and teachers are available to partner with you! You are not alone. Other parents can be a HUGE support as well.

Suggestions for dads

While more dads are getting involved in teaching their kids at home, in most homes, the mom is the primary co-teacher in our University-Model® schools. Regardless, supportive, involved fathers are key to a family flourishing in this model. Often the mom forms close connections with others at the school as well; but dads should jump in and get involved, too. Get to know the other dads. Get involved in service projects. Join your wife in this endeavor. Be a team player with her. This model of schooling is hard work. Hard does not mean wrong, however.

If your wife is struggling to stay above water in her role at home, don't automatically assume that the model does not work for your family. Make time for her to talk with you, and listen attentively to her. She may just need to know that you understand and value what she is doing. Pray with her. Perhaps on hard days, offer to bring dinner home. When your child is giving their mom a hard time at home, step in as the disciplinarian. Support your wife.

One great benefit of this model of education is the flexibility it provides. If Mom has too heavy of a load, Dad can pick up the slack by teaching a subject or two to their young children — even if it takes place in the evening. My husband, a math teacher, often helps our grandkids with their math assignments. My son-in-law Peter enjoys reading the history selections with his young children. He also helps with their daily reading assignments. With four kids in this model — three of whom are still in younger grades, his help in this area is vital.

In the middle and high school years, dads should be taking on more and more of the discipleship role and deliberately loving their kids during a time when their lives can feel turbulent and unsettling. The constant love and support of a father can make all the difference for the children as well as alleviating a burden of concern from their moms.

The Benefits

CHAPTER EIGHT

We Are Better Together: Here's Why

Parents are primary, but they do not have to be solitary. [20]

—Dr. John Turner

len and I began dating when we were seniors in college. I loved that he was working with youth in a local church and that he came from a close-knit family. As a married couple, we worked with youth — both as educators and in various ministries such as Young Life. As educators, we began to grow disillusioned, however, as we watched the eroding influence of parents in the schools in which we worked. My initial interest in Veritas Academy had to do with the enhanced parental role they espoused. I remember listening — with intrigue — as the founders of Veritas Academy spoke about their vision for this unique, hybrid model of education they were preparing to launch. A spark of hope rose within me that maybe — just maybe — this model would prove to be a school that authentically valued, supported and partnered together with parents.

While my heart was drawn to the ideas shared by the founders, I initially resisted the pull. Hadn't I just proclaimed that I would never jump into education again, especially into a school that was just starting up? Back in Oregon, leading a developing school had left me worn out and discouraged. It's why I proclaimed with certainty — as we moved from the west coast to Texas — that I not only was leaving Oregon but also the educational world for good. However, at this meeting, I began to wonder if perhaps this new model could become a true partnership with Christian families — one in which the parents were authentically valued in the journey of education.

This led me to apply for the head of school position at Veritas Academy. The application itself was so long that it would have weeded out most applicants. I certainly was tempted to toss it aside; but because of an unexpected surgery, I had the time and space to fill out the tediously long paperwork while I recuperated. God certainly has ways to keep us on His chosen path! I sent off the application with minimal enthusiasm; but three months later, I was offered the position. I signed on for a two-year contract — certain I would retire at the end of that period.

Seventeen years later, I am still at it. My experiences at Veritas Academy have been notably challenging yet exceptionally fulfilling and life-giving. Why am I still there when I envisioned retiring years ago? It comes down to the fact that I love this model of education and I am thrilled with what I see taking place. Together we are stronger. And better. Parents are primary, but they don't have to walk alone as they rear and educate their children. Instead the school and home join hands in a unique synergy devoted to training children together in a model in which academics and faith are not separate silos. The African proverb — *if you want to go fast, go alone; if you want to go far, go together* — holds great wisdom!

I have seen hundreds of students and families impacted, including my family. Each year I receive testimonies like this one, which is from a parent whose children attend Veritas Prep in Tucson. Her story paints a beautiful picture of what is taking place in families within our schools across this nation:

"Outside of Christ, our schooling choice has been the single most important

decision my husband and I have made in rearing our children Biblically. As we currently watch our oldest child walk through her senior year and get ready for college, the most valuable gift that the UMS model has given to us is time. With her getting ready to leave our home in a year, we treasure every home day we have together. This is not to minimize the academic and spiritual education the school has given us. It has been beyond our family's expectations. But the time we have gained with each of our children because of this model of schooling will be the true treasure we walk away with. It is one of the hardest things we've ever done, but it has also born the most fruit. The relationship my husband and I have with our kids is truly exceptional. This form of education is challenging; but it is the good, hard work. In fact, it is the best work we've ever done. We will be forever grateful to our UMS school for providing that for us and for our family."

You may be wondering what the long-term benefits are of joining a University-Model® community. While these benefits are a reality in our schools across this nation, the remainder of this chapter focuses largely on examples from Veritas Academy, where I have personally experienced and learned from this model.

A vision for students

Each year when I watch seniors walk across the stage and become graduates, I grow inspired. I see students who, in younger years, regularly challenged their parents and teachers; but they became inspirational leaders among their peers. I see students, who struggled academically, grow well-prepared to thrive in college. I see young men and women, who previously had questioned even the existence of God, willing to stand up boldly for their faith and Christian beliefs. I am gratified by watching our students learn to love God as they gain a true knowledge of Him and then want to grow to become more like Him.

The highest award a Veritas Academy student can receive at graduation is to be selected as the Veritas Valiant. The Veritas Valiant Creed, written by Jef Fowler, paints a portrait of a Veritas graduate that we hope all students aspire towards. It is our end goal in mind — the desired outcomes we want to see take place in our students' lives as they mature into adults. (You can find a copy of it in Appendix B.) From Kindergarten on, students and parents are reminded of the characteristics described in this creed. They include qualities such as becoming a humble, thankful, grateful child of God; a selfless servant-leader, prepared, assured and poised; a champion of justice; an attentive observer and industrious doer; a friend of the Almighty and much more.

Jef reminds our students that they are to *"focus on — and cultivate mastery over — the only three things in this world that they alone completely control: their attitude, their effort and their tongue."* He explains that their attitude determines the joy and satisfaction they find in life and, at the same time, can limit their possibilities. Their effort determines where they will reside within that realm of possibilities; yet their tongue has the power to destroy — in an instant — what they have spent countless hours building. I never tire of hearing him proclaim this truth. It's why I dedicated Chapter Four to words and their impact on our attitudes and actions.

Also, Jef calls for students to lead with the heart for the betterment of others and to do everything with a spirit of excellence. In University-Model® schools across our nation, school leaders set similar standards for students to strive for. When a community of like-minded parents and educators link arms together to raise up students — with a commitment to seek God in all things on behalf of all students, worthy things begin to take place within many.

While kids grow up and mature in a variety of settings, I consider this model of education to be especially effective in reaching the hearts of students. With a shared mission between school and home, students grow not only academically but also spiritually and emotionally. I am reminded of Weston (all names changed), who enrolled as a 10-year-old boy enamored with little else besides video games but who graduated as a connected leader among his peers with a strong worth ethic and virtuous character to back it up. I remember Cameron who, as an eighth grader, was unmotivated to work at anything. He walked into our school building each morning looking downcast and refusing to engage all day long. Yet four years later, he graduated with confidence and went on to successfully navigate college and life beyond. I remember Carly, who was riddled with anxiety until her junior year, when she read through Romans and came to the realization that her salvation rested in Jesus alone and not in her performance. Her collegiate life and beyond are testimonies to the continued and enduring work of Jesus in her heart. I still connect with Noelle, who as a young teen was scared and troubled with serious emotional issues. Today she is a successful doctor, walking in a vibrant faith. I am reminded of students, who felt rejected in younger grades, grow to become respected members of their classes and students, who questioned the validity of the Bible, come to an unwavering faith.

I see the lives of parents touched as well as they grow in their relationship with their children through the journey of walking with like-minded people, who are willing to hold each other accountable. I see marriages grow stronger as Mom and Dad learn to work together in partnership with a school who sets the standards *in rearing up winsome witnesses for Christ — in word and in deed.*

Academic outcomes

While I see numerous lifelong benefits for students and families in this model of education, I will begin by briefly describing academic ones. Each certified University-Model® school is automatically accredited through Cognia as part of systemwide accreditation. Therefore, parents can be assured that strong academic standards are in place. Students in our schools — across the nation — perform exceptionally well on college entrance exams, enroll in colleges and universities of their choosing and flourish in their collegiate endeavors.

Not only do students gain a solid foundation of knowledge, but they also develop lifelong skills that set up future success. For example, for students to succeed in this model, they must become self-directed learners. While they are instructed by teachers during part of each week, they also learn to apply what they learn to self-initiated study and application the rest of the week. Having led my grandchildren through this model, I see, firsthand, the growth of this taking place in all of them. They are becoming *"industrious doers, propelled by their own initiative"* as they advance through the grades.

(Italics are from the Veritas Academy Valiant Creed.)

Mission-minded outcomes

I also see our students becoming *"courageous defenders who rise above their fears to uphold Truth."* As they grow in knowledge through the lens of a Biblical worldview, they grow confident in what they believe. They can become *well-informed of the past and, therefore, mindful of the future* and equipped to influence their culture wisely. We desire that they come to love what is good, true and beautiful, which intentionally are put before them. Their identities are forming roots in a foundation of truth, springing up out of whom God has created them to be. They are becoming *a man or woman after God's own heart, a faithful friend of the Almighty.*

Becoming is a key word here. Our students are not perfect. Nor do any of them fully attain the standards outlined in the Veritas Valiant Creed. Some push on the boundaries year after year. Others exacerbate their parents both at home and with how they behave at school. Just this week, a mom called me to say she was tired and weary and thinking of putting her kids into a traditional school option. She and her husband had been getting regular calls about their two adolescent sons who were getting into trouble on a weekly basis. As I listened and asked questions, she finally expressed her deepest worry, *"Do these calls mean the school is wanting our family to leave?"* She had assumed that we had given up on her boys, leaving her feeling hopeless and worn out. As I explained that these calls represent our desire to partner with them in holding their sons to a standard, her mindset changed. I encouraged her to regard these communications as a gift — the school's commitment that they are not alone in rearing their kids.

We are imperfect educators and imperfect parents rearing imperfect children in an imperfect world. But we trust a perfect God who is at work in our lives *"both to will and to work for his good pleasure"* (Philippians 2:13).

Family outcomes

A father came to me one day when his oldest son was in eighth grade. He worried that the time together — that this model afforded his family — was destroying his relationship with his son and even his other two children. He described how he and his son were living in constant conflict. As I listened, I saw fear driving this father — fear of letting go, of losing control, fear of parenting a teenager, fear of losing his relationship with his firstborn. I encouraged him to adjust to a different style of parenting with his growing son, and he took this challenge seriously. I observed him to go on to make intentional adjustments in his parenting style with all three of his children as they aged. Today all three have graduated from Veritas; and both parents remain in healthy, connected and influential relationships with them. His oldest son is married, successfully navigating a career and in close relationships with his parents.

A current father of five children recently wrote to me saying, *"At times, the University-Model® is very stressful and challenging for our family; but when things are not going as smoothly as we would hope, I always think back to why we fell in love with this model in the first place. We now have the opportunity to partner with other parents and teachers in rearing our kids to have a fervent heart for the Lord, and we are strengthening our family bonds by having this increased time together."*

University-Model® schools offer parents time with their kids. This time is not necessarily easy, however — not only because of the time investment but also because they can work through conflict and relational issues that crop up in the school days at home. To be successful in this model, both parents and students must commit to diligent effort as well as the willingness to strive towards healthy interactions as they work together. At the same time, parents are not alone in this journey. They partner with a school who holds them to standards and who journeys with them through the ups and downs of parenting. Teachers, coaches, school leaders all join together, forming a team of adults who partner together in rearing students.

These schools include the youngest of students through seniors in high school, often all participating on the same campuses as well as at home together — another valuable benefit of this model of education. Not only do siblings have time to work together during each week, but they have the space to work out differences and learn to value one another. I love how my 10-year-old grandson William looks up to his teenage brother Joey. They have spent countless hours together over the years, working on school subjects — with Joey helping William as needed. William, in turn, helps his younger cousins when they come to my house for the school days. They are learning how to thoughtfully consider one another, in work and in play, forming close, lasting relationships.

In addition, University-Model® schools are not just educating the minds of our students but also forming hearts and encouraging students to live by God's priorities. We believe that His priorities include marriage and family, so we aim to rear boys and girls — not just for a higher education and a career path but also to become husbands and fathers, wives and mothers. In today's world, this oddly feels somewhat countercultural! According to the Pew Research Center, millennials are marrying later or not getting married at all. Plus, a growing number are electing to not have children or putting it off for years down the road. My heart rejoices each time I hear of a new engagement among our graduates or the arrival of a new baby. I envision future years in which children of our graduates will enroll in our school, which could begin to happen very soon. Already, a few of our graduates have returned as members of our faculty.

Belonging and connection outcomes

In a traditional school, parents send kids off to school five days a week and are largely free of the responsibility to educate them. Those who opt to fully homeschool take on the full responsibility, including being accountable for what to teach, how to teach, the pacing and deadlines. A University-Model® school is built on partnership — with each side being faithful in their roles and holding each other accountable. No silos. No hiding. This partnership nurtures community and a sense of belonging with others who are walking together in this important journey of rearing up the next generation. In this model, we walk neither dependently nor independently but interdependently in unified purpose.

This purpose is countercultural. University-Model® schools strive to conform young souls to a world with divine meaning and purpose; while the progressive culture encourages them to conform a meaningless, purposeless world to their needs and desires. These contrasting visions of reality result in contrasting visions of education and contrasting cultures. What children learn — and the environment in which they learn — matters greatly! Children and adults tend to acquire the characteristics of the culture by which they are surrounded. In other words, our moral consciousness is very much influenced and shaped by the communities to which they belong.

Still — even in our schools, churches and homes — the values and ideas of the prevailing culture continually seep in via technology. Plugging the holes is an impossible challenge, so instead we must prepare each of our children to stand strong in the face of the flow of misinformation. In partnering together, we form not a "bubble" but a sanctuary in which children are taught in countercultural ways and learn to engage the culture with a worldview rooted in God's Truth.

I often hear from parents, whose children attend a University-Model® school. Many of those parents, whose students have graduated, share a common message. I received this email from a mom of a recent graduate. It sums up beautifully why our schools exist: to raise the next generation of well-educated disciples of Christ.

"When we first began the journey within the University Model®, I honestly had no scope of the impact it would have on us as a family and our children. We have enjoyed the gift of time and the joys of watching them flourish and grow. However, it wasn't until recently that we have really been able to see it all come full circle — to see why we chose this model and how it works for the life of a child. A few weeks ago, we took our oldest to college for the first time. He is our introverted child and was not sure he even wanted to step into this journey alone; but we reassured him of all he had learned, of all that he is and all that God has called him to be. In just a short amount of time, we have seen the fruit of the University Model®. Not only does he call or text every day to keep that connection with us, to tell us about his day, to share with us the joys of his experiences and ask us advice; but we also see him connecting in the church regularly, meeting new people, serving them and pouring into them already. He has also shared that his school experience has prepared him well for this time. We are blessed for many reasons by the model; but this, seeing the fruit when they leave us, brings a continuous joy to our hearts as parents."

Once a lifelong Oregonian, I never would have imagined leaving the clover-covered hills and forests of my childhood for what I perceived to be dry, hot, flat Texas. Yet my entire family now resides in Austin, Texas, where we walk out life together, rearing our family's next generation within a University-Model® community. At the start of this book, I shared how hunting for a rare four-leaf clover still stood out as a clear memory, symbolizing a lifelong search for true meaning and value in life. When we left Oregon, I assumed I also was leaving the world of education behind as well. Instead God moved me back into a different kind of school setting — one that is strengthening Christian families all around our nation and making a difference for God's kingdom. I consider it a deep joy to serve families within schools who value parents as primary yet partner with them in rearing up boys and girls in the paideia of the Lord. Together we are better!

Top 50 Tips for Setting Up Your School@Home Spaces

Courtesy of Veritas Moms

Compiled by Molly Ingram

This chapter contains the top 50 tips for setting up your school@home spaces. This list was compiled by Molly Ingram, whose two boys have attended Veritas Academy since preschool and are now in sixth and eighth grades. Not only is Molly a parent in our school; but she now serves as a faculty member, a board member and a member of our Family Ministry team. Her list is full of great ideas — courtesy of many moms who she surveyed.

1. Pray for God's vision for your school@home environment.

2. Have a bin for saving completed/graded assignments.

3. Don't throw away any papers/work until the end of the school year.

4. At the end of the year, decide what to keep and what to recycle.

5. Think through places to read, write, keep books/supplies and complete projects.

6. Use cubbies to organize books and supplies.

7. Keep all technology in the main area of your house for good visibility.

8. Kitchen and dining tables make great workspaces, especially for projects.

9. Read on the couch or a comfy chair.

10. Read/study by the pool.

11. Read/go over notes in a hammock.

12. Read/review in a window seat or another special nook in your home.

13. Read/listen to read-alouds on a bean bag chair.

14. For all those SR-credit classes, save all your tests because they may need to be turned in at the end of the year.

15. Have a clipboard for each student's Homework Plans and other important papers.

16. Keep a box/cup of school supplies with pens, pencils, erasers and tabs that you only get out for school time.

17. Plastic roller bins/drawers are great for storage. Use the bottom drawer(s) for completed/graded assignments. Roll the unit into a closet when not in use.

18. Large magnetic white boards are a must-have.

19. Listen to skip counting, songs, states, capitals, Latin songs, etc. in the car. Create a playlist, so they're handy to access.

20. Have a basket for all your math "stuff" like flashcards, manipulatives, etc.

21. Have a basket for language arts "stuff" like phonogram cards.

22. Don't worry about having a dedicated school room. It's not necessary. Your "school room" absolutely could be your kitchen table and a rolling cart.

23. Having a dedicated school room is a-okay! Do what works for your family.

24. A dining room cabinet or hutch can make a great school storage area.

25. Make lunches the night before your school@home day, so you have one less thing to do.

26. Make the exact same lunch every school@home day.

27. Keep dinner super easy on school@home days.

28. Home days can be crockpot days.

29. Prepare for your week on Saturday or Sunday.

30. You also could prep for your school week on Mondays and run your errands on Wednesdays.

31. Put assignments in file folder bins, label a hanging folder per subject and off you go.

32. Keep a couple of extra poster boards handy.

33. Include your kids in the workspace prep process.

34. Use magazine boxes to organize books and teacher manuals.

35. Small dry-erase boards/markers are great for practicing math problems, spelling, etc.

36. Have a basket for all the "extras." At the end of the day, put that basket in its designated spot on the shelf to keep things tidy.

37. Make sure everything has a place.

38. Think about a space to display projects.

39. Make a laminated checklist of subjects for your student to check off what has been done.

40. It's okay to do work outside. Keep your workspace mindset flexible.

41. A bookcase with tubs can help you stay organized.

42. Use that flexible schedule to go to museums, exhibits, outings, etc.

43. Use workboxes in the younger grades to help with pacing and organization.

44. Give each kid a shelf for their school@home things.

45. Get a good pencil sharpener. This is crucial!

46. A secretary desk is a good option for school@home storage.

47. Do memory work or verbal quizzing on the trampoline.

48. Spread a blanket out in the yard on a pretty day for schoolwork.

49. Depending on the age of your students, go "off campus" and do school at the local library, coffee shop or park.

50. BUY PRINTER INK. LOTS. OF. IT. :-)

The Veritas
Valiant Award

Preamble

In addition to Veritas Academy's recognitions for the good man speaking well — our *Senior Thesis Laureate* — and the most exemplary scholars — our *Valedictorian and Salutatorian,* we also recognize one who leaves behind a legacy of leading with the heart in the betterment of self and others — our *Veritas Valiant.*

As educators, parents and mentors, it is incumbent upon us to challenge each young person entrusted to our care to focus on — and cultivate mastery over — the only three things in this world that they, and they alone, completely control: their attitude, their effort and their tongue. Their **Attitude** determines the joy and satisfaction they find in life; and it defines — and especially limits — their possibilities. The cynic has little potential. Their **Effort** determines where they will reside within that realm of possibilities. Ambition — or perhaps more accurately, *desire* — is the fuel of the engine of effort. Either selfish desire or noble ambition will drive effort — though the latter more broadly and sustainably. But regardless the motive — noble or otherwise, desire without effort is without impact. And, finally, their **Tongue** has the power to undo it all. It's the match that most of us use to destroy — in an instant — what we have spent countless hours building.

In many ways, the Veritas Valiant creed is simply a codification of the *attitudes* and *efforts* — and their underlying desires — along with the *words* behind a life that produces meaningful substance, influence and fulfillment. This award recognizes a person whose life well lived commands the respect and appreciation of those around him. It's for the broadly influential person who — in his or her time at Veritas — had the heart and ability to bring out the best in others while challenging all to become even better, continuing a legacy of sacrificial servant-leadership at the academy.

Creed

The Veritas Valiant Award, the academy's highest honor, is meant to acknowledge a graduating senior, whose life is marked not just by intellect and accomplishment but also by effective leadership, a spirit of excellence and personal virtue. The award is conferred upon one who possesses and pursues the aspirational, noble qualities we desire to see embodied in a person of whom others would remark, "Now there's a Veritas Man/Woman." That ideal is…

- the good man speaking well;

- the courageous defender who rises above his fear to uphold Truth and protect the vulnerable;

- the selfless, servant-leader — prepared, assured and poised;

- the tenacious competitor — gracious in victory, resilient in defeat;

- the contagiously joyful, hopeful, positive encourager of others;

- the loyal, honorable, reliable man of constant character;

- the curiously attentive observer and industrious doer — propelled by his initiative, tempered by his good judgment and self-control;

- the passionately purposeful, ambitious, adventurous spirit — fully alive and engaged;

- the wise, well-read, lifelong learner — ordered in reason and desires, delighting in wonder;

- the compassionate, kind and generous helper of the hurting;

- the irrepressible visionary — informed of the past, mindful of the future, master of the moment in pursuit of his calling;

- the daring dreamer and maker of mistakes who humbly makes right those mistakes — risking failure, owning error, diligently repairing the damage;

- the patient, sincere listener — discerner of the heart and intents of others;

- the witty, inquisitive, contemplative soul — appreciative of silence and solitude;

- the champion of justice but abounding in grace and mercy;

- the lover of all that is good, true and beautiful, drinking deeply of it;

- the thankful, grateful child of God and winsome witness of Christ — in word and in deed; a man after God's own heart; faithful friend of the Almighty.

Our Valiant Award designee is a worthy ambassador for the institution — one we are proud to bear the imprimatur of Veritas Academy.

Identity Statements: Core Values for the Family

Developed for Families by Veritas Academy Family Ministries

This list of identity statements — or principles to live by — is not intended to be exhaustive. Rather it defines the key ideals — inherent in a school and home — that form a culture in which faith and growth flourish. They establish wise practices for parents and educators in rearing up knowledgeable, virtuous men and women who will stand firmly in their Christian faith and identity.

1. We put our trust and hope in Jesus Christ, who is the anchor of our souls.

    a. Our trust and security shall be rooted — not in our performance for Him but in the redemptive work of our loving God and what He accomplished for us on the cross. *"...Christ in you, the hope of glory"* (Colossians 1:27^{cd}).

    b. God is the Architect and the Master Planner. His ways are greater than ours, and He accomplishes His purposes in us out of love. Therefore, we will turn to Him for guidance and direction and not rely on our ways. *"Unless the LORD builds the house, those who build it labor in vain..."* (Psalm 127:1). The word *house* here refers to a family lineage and not a building.

    c. We instill hope and courage in our children — that God has called them to "such a season as this" and He will equip them to walk uprightly in it. We teach our children to not fear the present but to maintain *eternity in their hearts*. *"He only is my rock and my salvation, my fortress; I shall not be shaken. On God rests my salvation and my glory; my mighty rock, my refuge is God"* (Psalm 62:6-7).

d. We encourage parents to rear their children out of faith and not fear by trusting in God and leaning daily on the Holy Spirit. *"May the God of hope fill you with all joy and peace in believing, so that by the power of the Holy Spirit you may abound in hope"* (Romans 15:13).

e. We purpose to pray. *"Do not be anxious about anything, but in everything by prayer and supplication with thanksgiving let your requests be made known to God"* (Philippians 4:6).

2. We desire to love God and allow His love to flow through us to others.

a. We recognize the greatest commandment as our overarching mission in everything we do. *"You shall love the LORD your God with all your heart and with all your soul and with all your mind. This is the great and first commandment. And a second is like it: You shall love your neighbor as yourself"* (Matthew 22:37-39).

b. We will consider each person as someone God has made on purpose, with purpose and for purpose. *"I praise you, for I am fearfully and wonderfully made. Wonderful are your works; my soul knows it very well"* (Psalm 139:14).

c. We look for ways to serve others. *"For you were called to freedom, brothers. Only do not use your freedom as an opportunity for the flesh, but through love serve one another. For the whole law is fulfilled in one word: 'You shall love your neighbor as yourself'"* (Galatians 5:13-14).

3. We purpose to live virtuous lives — with our strength coming from Christ; and we purpose to guide our children to do the same. We govern our daily lives by:

a. **Justice:** To make right, to be morally fair. *"To do righteousness and justice is more acceptable to the LORD than sacrifice"* (Proverbs 21:3).

b. **Prudence:** To govern and discipline oneself by the use of reason and well-thought-out decisions. *"Every prudent man acts with knowledge, but a fool flaunts his folly"* (Proverbs 13:16).

c. **Temperance:** To be habitually moderate in the indulgences of the appetites or passions. *"Every athlete exercises self-control in all things. They do it to receive a perishable wreath, but we an imperishable"* (1 Corinthians 9:25).

d. **Fortitude:** To be strong in the face of adversity or difficulty; to stand up for what is right in the sight of God; to have courage or grit. *"For God gave us a spirit not of fear but of power and love and self-control"* (2 Timothy 1:7).

4. We focus on practices that reach and influence the hearts of our children rather than settling for behavior management approaches that focus merely on external actions.

a. We are about heart change over outward compliance. We desire not only to inform our children's minds but also to form their hearts.

b. We recognize that the desires of the heart drive choices. Knowing what's right is not enough. Our children must come to desire from within what is true, good and beautiful. *"Keep your heart with all vigilance, for from it flow the springs of life"* (Proverbs 4:23). *"The good person out of the good treasure of his heart produces good, and the evil person out of his evil treasure produces evil, for out of the abundance of the heart his mouth speaks"* (Luke 6:45).

c. Because children need to develop self-control that is not reliant on external controls, we purpose not to micromanage our kids or overly control their behaviors but to encourage their need to grow self-control.

d. We model and expect integrity — people who are honest, trustworthy, reliable and dependable — whether others are watching or not. *"Whoever walks in integrity walks securely, but he who makes his ways crooked will be found out"* (Proverbs 10:9).

5. We believe that parents should be the primary influence for their children and embrace their parental authority in loving ways. To that end, we discipline our children with an approach that is redemptive and not punitive in nature.

   a. We embrace the concept of grace yet hold steadfastly to and expect wise, strong standards. *"And the Word became flesh and dwelt among us, and we have seen his glory, glory as of the only Son from the Father, full of grace and truth"* (John 1:14).

   b. We hold to virtuous standards, but we do not use shame as an approach in training our kids. While they must come to feel the weight of their poor choices (guilt), they must not consider themselves undeserving of — or beyond — God's love and forgiveness (shame).

6. We view growth as a daily decision and complacency as never becoming an option.

   a. Growth and change are lifetime endeavors, especially in our faith. *"For this very reason, make every effort to supplement your faith with virtue, and virtue with knowledge, and knowledge with self-control, and self-control with steadfastness, and steadfastness with godliness, and godliness with brotherly affection, and brotherly affection with love. For if these qualities are yours and are increasing, they keep you from being ineffective or unfruitful in the knowledge of our Lord Jesus Christ"* (2 Peter 1:5-8).

   b. We foster a growth mindset in our children as opposed to a fixed mindset.

    i. Growth Mindset: The belief that your basic qualities are things you can cultivate through effort; that a person's true potential is unknown and will develop passion, hard work and training.

    ii. Fixed Mindset: The belief that your basic qualities are fixed and unchangeable; that one, therefore, should only pursue interests that come easily.

    iii. We expect our children to learn how to do hard things well.

c. We advocate for excellence but not perfection. God is *perfecting* us, but only Christ was the *perfect* man. To that end, we treat mistakes as learning opportunities and failures as a means to learn resiliency.

d. We are all in need of discipleship and mentorship.

    i. We need each other. *"Iron sharpens iron, and one man sharpens another"* (Proverbs 27:17).

    ii. We shall strive for personal humility and mutual encouragement. *"For everyone who exalts himself will be humbled, and he who humbles himself will be exalted"* (Luke 14:11). *"The reward for humility and fear of the LORD is riches and honor and life"* (Proverbs 22:4).

    iii. We shall develop a culture of openness by which parents and students will admit their mistakes without fear of rejection — one in which it's OK to be broken.

e. We endeavor to, and encourage one another to, bear the fruit of the Spirit – love, joy, peace, patience, kindness, goodness, faithfulness, gentleness, self-control.

7. We foster and model a grateful, forgiving culture.

a. We choose to be grateful *in* the midst of all circumstances, knowing that God is sovereign and in control of our lives. *"In everything give thanks; for this is the will of God in Christ Jesus for you"* (1 Thessalonians 5:18).

b. We do not grumble, complain or gossip. Rather we speak with others directly and honestly.

c. We seek to edify each other and our community by sharing the all-surpassing peace of Christ, avoiding slander, gossip and discord and refusing to act out of selfish ambition, arrogance, anger or a complaining spirit.

d. We model forgiveness with others instead of anger and bitterness. We do not provoke our children in anger. *"Fathers, do not provoke your children to anger, but bring them up in the discipline and instruction of the Lord"* (Ephesians 6:4).

e. We do our part to bring about reconciliation. *"If possible, so far as it depends on you, live peaceably with all"* (Romans 12:18).

8. We purpose to develop hearts and minds at rest amidst a culture full of distractions.

a. We choose to be attentive to the things of God over the things of this world. *"Be still, and know that I am God..."* (Psalm 46:10).

b. We participate in the spiritual practices of prayer, Scripture reading and meditation on God's Word.

c. We stay informed about our children's use of digital devices, communicate with them regularly about wise use and be prepared to address inappropriate contact, content and conduct.

Recommended Resources

F ollowing is a list of resources that have proven to support our mission at Veritas Academy and the culture we want to promote. In no way is this list meant to be complete; rather it includes some resources that have proven to have a strong impact within our schools' communities.

Books by Individuals Within the University-Model® Community:

- *Character Driven College Preparation* by Dr. John William Turner, Jr. The author explains how our schools bring together the best attributes of traditional schooling with the best attributes of home schooling and integrate them into one model. The ultimate goal is that of producing wholesome, competent men and women of character who make a positive difference in the next generation.

- *Make It a Place of Springs* by Michael Chrasta. This book is a mandate and a guide for promoting a vigorous culture of life in Christian school communities. In clear and succinct short essays, the author explores the foundations of this culture, the role of prayer in producing it and the ways all members of the community can nourish and sustain it.

- *Free to Parent* by Ellen Schuknecht & Erin MacPherson. This book ministers to parents by helping them escape the trap of lifeless, rule-driven parenting to joyfully growing and nurturing their children's hearts.

- *Put the Disciple into Discipline: Parenting with Love and Limits* by Erin MacPherson & Ellen Schuknecht. This book gives parents the tools they need to disciple their kids through trying discipline situations. With these tools, parents can guide their kid's hearts towards the God who loves them.

Parenting Books:

- *8 Great Smarts* by Kathy Koch, Ph.D. The author provides a clear description of the eight kinds of intelligences and how to nurture them in your children.

- **Other Great Resources** by Kathy Koch, Ph,D. the founder and president of Celebrate Kids, Inc. and a cofounder of Ignite the Family.

  - *Five to Thrive*

  - *Screens and Teens*

  - *No More Perfect Kids* (& Jill Savage)

  - *Encouraged* Podcast

- *Loving Your Kids on Purpose* by Danny Silk. The author integrates Love & Logic approaches with spiritual principles by teaching parents how to train children to manage their freedoms and protect their important heart-to-heart relationships.

- *Boundaries with Kids: How Healthy Choices Grow Healthy Kids* by Dr. Henry Cloud and Dr. John Townsend. The authors provide the help and guidance you need for rearing your kids to take responsibility for their actions, attitudes and emotions. Also by the same authors: *Boundaries with Teens: When to Say Yes, How to Say No*

- *Collapse of Parenting* by Leonard Sax, M.D., Ph.D. Drawing on more than 25 years of experience, Dr. Sax makes a convincing case that, if we are to help our children avoid the pitfalls of an increasingly complicated world, we must reassert authority as parents.

- *Mindsets: The New Psychology of Success* by Carol S. Dweck, Ph.D. In her fascinating book, the author shows how success in school, work, sports, the arts and almost every area of human endeavor can be influenced dramatically by how we think about our talents and abilities.

- *Teaching from Rest: A Homeschooler's Guide to Unshakeable Peace* by Sarah Mackenzie. In this practical, faith-based and inspirational book, the author addresses how stress, worry and anxiety get in the way of peace and shares how she was able to bring restful learning to her (six) children.

Books about Biblical Worldview and Culture:

- *The Rise and Triumph of the Modern Self* by Carle R. Trueman. The author provides a deeply informed account of the modern self and how it has shaped our cultural battles.

- *Knowledge of the Holy* by A.W. Tozer. Tozer discusses the attributes of God in ways that strengthen and deepen the spiritual life and restores the Christian concept of God to the center of life.

- *A Practical Guide to Culture: Helping the Next Generation Navigate Today's World* by John Stonestreet and Brett Kunkle. With Biblical clarity, this practical go-to manual is designed to equip kids to rise above the culture.

- *Another Gospel: A Lifelong Christian Seeks Truth in Response to Progressive Christianity* by Alisa Childers. If you or someone you love has encountered the ideas of progressive Christianity and aren't sure how to respond, Alisa's journey will show you how to determine — and rest in — what's unmistakably true.

- *Beyond Biblical Immersion: Immersing You and Your Students in a Biblical Worldview* by Roger C. S. Erdvig. In this book, the author explains why Biblical worldview development is the central key to accomplishing your school's mission and practical strategies for how to transform your school into an immersive, Biblical worldview environment.

- *Love the Body* by Nancy R. Pearcey. The author goes right to the big issues of our times, considering what makes humans valuable in the first place.

ENDNOTES

1. Gloria Naylor, *Goodreads* www.goodreads.com/quote/803240

2. John Stonestreet, *The Rise and Triumph of the Modern Self: Sex, Identity, and the Image of God*, Breakpoint, Colson Center for Christian Worldview, 04-21-21. www.breakpoint.org, pg. 8

3. Carl R. Trueman, *The Rise and Triumph of the Modern Self*, Crossway, 2020, pg. 9

4. *ibid.,* pg. 12

5. Debbie Lord, "Billy Graham Quotes: He Made Christian Principles Accessible to Millions", *The Atlanta Journal-Constitution*, Publisher: Donna B. Hall, 02-21-2018, www.ajc.org, pg. 17

6. A.W. Tozer, *The Knowledge of The Holy*, Harper & Row, 1961, pg. 20-21

7. *ibid.,* pg. 23

8. *ibid.,* pg. 35

9. *ibid.,* pg. 58-59

10. Dane Ortlund, *GENTLE and LOWLY,* Crossway, 2020, pg. 24-25

11. *ibid.,* pg. 32-33

12. Dallas Willard, *The Great Omission: Essential Teachings on Discipleship*, Harper One, 2006, pg. 28

13. John Piper, *The Image of God, Desiring God,* John Piper, 03-01-1971, www.desiringgod.org, pg. 31

14. John Stonestreet and Brett Kunkle, *A Practical Guide to Culture*, David C Cook, 2017, 2020, pg. 34

15. J. Warner Wallace, *Cold Case Christianity*, David C Cook, 2013, pg. 34

16. Alisa Childers, *Another Gospel*, TYNDALE, 2020, pg. 34

17. David Platt, *Follow Me: A Call to Die. A Call to Live*, TYNDALE, 2013, pg. 41

18. Dr. John William Turner Jr., *Character-Driver College Preparation*, NAUMS, Inc., 2017, pg. 43

19. *ibid.*, pg. 43

20. *ibid.*, pg. 147

21. Eugene H. Peterson, *The Message: The Bible in Contemporary Language*, NavPress, 1993, 2002, 2018, pg. 43

22. Jim Wilder & Michel Hendricks, *The Other Half of Church*, Moody Publishers, 2020, pg. 50

23. Ruth Schwenk, *Warrior Moms, You're Raising Arrows, The Better Mom*, Ruth Schwenk, 07-27-2021, www.thebettermom.com, pg. 56

24. Vern L. Bengston, *Families and Faith: How Religion Is Passed Down across Generations*, OXFORD University Press, 2013, pg. 57

25. C. S. Lewis, *Mere Christianity*, Barbour and Company, Inc., 1943, 1945, 1952, pg. 59

26. *ibid.*, pg. 65

27. Geoffrey Bromley, *God & Marriage*, William B. Eerdman Publishing Company, 1980, pg. 67

28. Charles Capps, *The Tongue: A Creative Force*, Capps Publishing, 1976, pg. 73

29. Joyce Meyer, *CHANGE Your Words, CHANGE Your Life*, Hodder & Stoughton, 2012, pg. 75

30. Mo Petty, *Apples of Gold*, C. R. Gibson Company, 1972, pg. 81

31. C. S. Lewis, *The Chronicles of NARNIA*, Harper Collins, 1956, pg. 87

32. Dr. James C. Dobson, *The New Strong-Willed Child*, TYNDALE, 2017, pg. 89

33. Ken Poirot, *Mentor Me,* Dog Ear Publishing, 2014, pg. 94

34. Kathy Koch, PhD., *8 Great Smarts,* Moody Publishers, 2015, pg. 96

35. Charles Spurgeon, *Quotes,* www.quotes.net/quote/17668, pg. 99

36. Rev. Dr. Martin Luther King, Jr., *GoodReads,* www.goodreads,com/quotes/199214, pg. 99

37. Henry Ward Beecher, *BrainyQuote,* www.brainyquote.com/quotes/163037, pg. 100

38. Michael Law, *GoodReads,* www.goodreads.comquotes/472698, pg. 109

39. Michael de Montaigne, Forbes, *Forbes Press Room,* www.forbes.com/quotes/6829, pg. 121

40. Dr. Neil T. Anderson, *Who I Am in Christ,* Bethany House, 2001, pg. 123

41. *ibid.,* pg. 128

42. Lauren DiMaria, *Attractive Teens Don't Have More Self-Esteem Than Peers,* VeryWell Mind, 04-25-2020, www.verywellmind.com, pg. 125

43. Winston Churchill, *TreasureQuotes,* www.treasurequotes.com/quotes/there-is-no-doubt-that-it-is-around-family, pg. 131

44. John C. Maxwell, *Today Matters,* Time Warner Book Group, 2004, pg. 135

ABOUT THE AUTHOR

 **Ellen Schuknecht's** experience spans traditional public and private school education. She mentors families at Veritas Academy in Austin, Texas, and supports other schools as the Family Ministry coordinator for University Model® Schools International (UMSI). Her most important time each week are the two school days spent with her grandchildren at her home. Ellen has co-authored several books on parenting and education, including *A Spiritual Heritage: Connecting Kids and Grandkids to God and Family* co-authored with her husband, Glen. The Schuknechts have been guests of Focus on the Family; and they reside in Manchaca, Texas, near their adult children and grandchildren.